My Bare Naked Truth

One Butterfly at a Time

By: **Lori Welton**

Copyright © 2024

Published by: Book Publish Pro

DEDICATION

To The Daughter I Never Had

Vibrations from the voices around me jolted my body back and forth while remaining secure inside my warm and cozy place. Hearing laughter, my mouth began to curve slightly. Noises began to enlighten my ears. What are these moving parts that are attached to me? My existence is only of God's will. Will I ever see the other side? Many have come and gone from this space. Tragically, the answer came the next morning. The contentment and security were gone, and there were no more sounds or moving body parts for the 28-week-old baby. All the woman had left was a dead, empty womb when it was all over. Sadness, guilt, and depression set in once again. At this point in her life, she experienced several miscarriages, none of which developed to the point of connection or knowing the sex like this one. The woman and her unborn girl bonded daily until God decided to take her home. A few years later, God blessed her with two healthy and strong boys, who turned out to be amazing life lessons within themselves and continued to enrich her life. But Ashley Nichole was the daughter she never had. For years, the woman journaled messages and thoughts to share with her every day, all about her struggles, life lessons, finding love, self-love, and battling her demons. She began helping many young women by telling her life stories and giving advice. Now, it's time to reach beyond her inner circle to touch more people and give encouragement for a happier life. It is time for her to write about the experiences that have led her to a better life for herself. Ashley, this is for you!

Table of Contents

Introduction 1

My Foundation 3

The Beginning of My Nightmares 8

They Will Always Be With Me 12

The Cycle Gets Broken 17

New Beginnings 21

My Cinderella Story 26

My Great Awakening 30

My Second Chance at Love 34

Our Bombs and Battlefields 38

Beauty and the Beast 42

Bark Street 46

Returning to Myself 51

Freedom From my Unwanted Guests 55

Taking Back my Sunshine 60

Confession is Good For The Soul 64

Building My Bridges Back 68

My Proud And Not So Proud Moments 72

Thank You For My Anger 77

Finding Peace Within My Body 82

Connecting With My Chakras 86

From Dreams To Reality 91

Introduction

"Perhaps the butterfly is proof that you can go through a great deal of darkness, yet still become something beautiful."

Beau Taplin

Smell the salty air as it blows through the coastal sand dunes. With the intensity of the bright sun radiating down, you feel the heat from the sparkling white sand between your toes. Looking above the crystal blue sky, you see it filled with a variety of gorgeous birds gliding around. In the distance is an elephant stumbling as he tries to walk down the beach; look closer, and you see a swarm of bees surrounding him. He begins to swat fiercely with his trunk back and forth, trying to keep them off him. As you look to the side of him, you notice beautiful butterflies fluttering around boxes, some half opened and some half closed, scattered around surrounded by lotus flowers. Shifting your attention to the other side of the beach, you see a little girl playfully bouncing up and down the shoreline. She was watching dolphins play in the water. As they jumped in and out of the water, you could hear her musical laugh echo across the waves. Suddenly she took off toward an old abandoned fun park. As she began running down the beach, she looked back and said, "Come find me!" As she enters the park, she heads into the house of mirrors. Following her inside, you become aware that every mirror is broken, with many different sad images of the girl displayed on each one. You begin to glance from mirror to mirror with confusion, and suddenly she vanishes. Your heart begins to race, searching for her, as you touch each mirror, realizing the faces switched to your reflections. You begin to panic and aimlessly glance in every direction for some kind of clue. Abruptly, a scared and trembling voice cries out and says to you, "Help find me!" You feel a sharp pain in your chest, which is familiar, as it rushes through the realization of a panic attack settling in from anxiety. This had become a common part of your daily life but never in your dreams. You close your eyes tightly and take a deep breath; when you open your eyes, all you see is darkness. As you begin to feel your way around the slick surfaces, a door opens; walking through it, you notice the sand between your toes is cold, not warm. The sun was no longer shining, and the sky was gloomy, with eagles and hawks flying over the still waters. There is the elephant trying to walk down the beach, but instead of fighting off bees, it was wasps swarming him, and there were no beautiful butterflies flying around him and only dead flowers along with the scattered half-opened and half-closed boxes with blood oozing from them. Horrified, you look away to the opposite side of the beach. Catching a glimpse of thrashing in the water, you move toward it to get a better look; there is the little girl crying and staring at crocodiles fighting with each other in the rough waters. As you draw near, she turns towards you and says, "Please find me before it's too late! Alarmed, you freeze, and black dust begins to swirl around you and carries it all away.

Waking up the next morning, with a golden sun rising over the horizon, piercing its glorious colors through the large windows in the house, an invitation to a new day was about to begin. As for the woman upstairs, she was lying in pitch darkness from the night before. Her eyes were tightly closed, her hands clutching the bedspread for dear life, sweating, and tears rolling down her face. Feeling overwhelmed by emotional turmoil from the nightmares of the night before and all the years in the past that had tortured her in her sleep, she was not ready to accept the invitation.

As the morning birds began to sing, she could hear the sound of mini drums from the woodpeckers tapping on the trees and the shuffling of her family stirring around downstairs. She knew it was time to get up; the people in her life were counting on her as they usually did every morning. Her mornings before used to be filled with anticipation for the day's agenda. Everyone looked forward to a day planned full of excitement, new adventures, and fun memories to be made, not to mention endless conversations about anything and everything. Most mornings, everyone would wake up rested from a good night's sleep, calm and ready to tackle the day together, but that hasn't been the case in years. Since the traumatic events and emotional stress that plagued the family over the past years, some never seemed affected; some have developed and matured from them, while others are still fighting their demons. She is one that is still fighting her demons, present and past. Her family now wakes up with their own agendas for the day. Kids were growing up, making their own choices, having their own plans for the day, and figuring out their own direction in life, which is healthy and natural. She and her husband were adjusting to the kids growing up and the many changes from their own life situations. Some of the changes were starting to come between them which left her puzzled and confused at times, while other changes helped them fully grow together. Life was changing and moving around her, and she was standing still, waking up from nightmares only to begin her mornings with a reluctant fear of anxiety because she knew when her feet hit the floor, the roller coaster from hell and the merry-go-round of doubt and fear was about to start. The woman upstairs is me, and my story must be told for the daughter I never had and anyone else who might share similar demons or changes that continue to arise in their lives. I know I am not alone in what I have gone through or am about to face. So, for me, I must express my story in a way that I find healing and understanding from my past so I can make my way clear toward my future. From my sad beginnings, you will hear my truth only to prove how I have turned my negative situations into positive ones through countless years of peeling off multiple layers of myself to reveal the amazing woman I am. If you are at a place in life where your past is tormenting your present and standing in your way to a better life, I encourage you to hear my story. Allow me to share with you as I would to the daughter I never had about my transformation.

CHAPTER ONE

My Foundation

"Children are like wet cement. Whatever falls on them makes an impression."

Dr. Hiam Ginnot

Regardless of whether or not I rested well the night before, my routine was to get up at 5:00 a.m. every morning. I would grab a cup of coffee and head outside to the front porch to observe nature, animals, and the day come alive, watching the sky introduce its array of colors to the sun as dawn began breaking through. This was my personal time before my family and the rest of the world joined my day. After taking in the outside world, I went inward through prayer, speaking out loud with Ashley, and spent time reading until my coffee was gone. Today, the topic of my daily readings was domestication. Intrigued by what I had read, I decided to have lunch at the community park to observe domestication firsthand. Allow me to share with you what I observed that day. There were a variety of animals hanging around; there were squirrels, deer, birds, and plenty of dogs, just to name a few. The park was flooded with people and children of all ages. Taking your attention over to a sandbox, you see several children between one to three years of age. Captivated by their laughter, you are drawn to watch their playful nature as they explore their huge imaginations to create their own fun and entertainment. Their eyes are wide and lively, and their animated actions invite you to gaze into their pleasure and enjoyment as you watch them interact with each other. Every so often, there is one that doesn't follow the rules and disrupts the play, but you notice how easily they all adjust, react, and move on as if nothing happened. Children at that age simply let go and live in the moment, but they are never really affected because only fun and happiness are all that matter to them. You begin to notice older children piling into the sandbox, watching with anticipation as this will change the whole dynamics of play for everyone in the sandbox. These children are around seven to ten years old. Once the older children start to engage, they shift the adventure towards their ideas and slowly take over. At first, this might seem natural, but when a different type of adventure is introduced, one or two begin to demand or force others to play their way; soon, no one wants to participate, and the enjoyment disappears. Instructions on how to speak and act and which toy to use make the younger children lose interest and resist playing in the sandbox because now no one is having fun anymore. The smaller children start bailing out as the older children quickly take over. What was once enjoyable to watch has turned sad to observe because little adults are beginning to emerge with their tempers, their firm demands, and plenty of their own self-directed fun. The leaders and followers are being created, and roles are being developed. A couple of older children begin to speak rudely and play aggressively. This affects everyone involved since attitudes and words change. As younger children always look up to older children as examples of how they should act or speak, this disruption has them exposed to another type of influence they must choose to follow or not. By watching their actions and attitudes, this could be good or bad, considering which one of those they decide to choose to follow. By listening and watching this scene take place, it is obvious which ones are affected by the older children because their faces appear sad, more serious, and mean and all of their smiles are gone. Love and fun come naturally to younger children since they are born with a sense of peace, so when that is taken away, they feel discouraged and unsafe. Their harmony and peace were replaced with chaos and conflict, along with much confusion on where the fun disappeared. When things in life disrupt our peace, we become lost and confused, especially when it disrupts the enjoyment we have been feeling. Children are no different. It's just harder for them to understand.

Drawing your attention to the animals in the park, you can see the difference between the ones that are domesticated and the ones that are not. Animals that live in the wild are not domesticated; they live free to follow their instincts and do as they please with no corrections from anyone. Domesticated animals are tamed, taught how to behave by punishment and reward, and converted to a certain way of living, which creates a dependence on their human. Children are domesticated much like animals; they are taught by the adults in their lives who have raised[h1] them on how to live, how to act, and how to play. They are conditioned by the same punishment and reward system on how to behave; this happens because they are just like sponges. They soak up the beliefs and social influences of the people and the environment that surrounds them. As a child, domestication is unavoidable due to the helplessness and guidance you need early on to thrive in the world; it's how you survive and make sense of what is happening around you. So much trust and faith from adults or peers are established for a child to feel safe and secure. When the children were exposed to a different type of domestication. They get a sense of uncertainty, which can be unsettling. The unfamiliarity of this new domestication or new examples is disturbing and unknown to them. If all of the children were domesticated exactly the same and behaved the same way, all would be good-natured, but this isn't the case because no two people are exactly alike and definitely not raised the same. It's not until years later one must decide and can break away from domestication to become one's own individual. This is where the problem occurs, and life gets messy. Domestication evolves from all types of people, some with healthy perspectives, some distorted by their circumstances, and all can be situational. Healthy behaviors can give solid, positive ways to interact with others, while negative behaviors can lead to mistreating others in bad ways. Emotional poison is to blame for this. Emotional poison is any bad emotions that someone feels either about themselves, another person, or a situation and has the need to release it but doesn't know how to. They might release it by intentionally pouring onto someone their hurt emotions in the attempt to only make themselves feel better, or by simply getting it out, which in turn leaves them unaware that what they released has the potential to stay with that person while they feel better getting it out. Without regard for how your actions play out or how they will affect others, the passing of this emotional poison is devastating, especially to a child. This can happen when contaminated people enter into our minds and space with all of their emotional poison and share it like a contagious virus. This can replace happiness and joy with dark clouds of doubt and fear instantly and if the children are not strong enough to handle the disruption, they are often left bewildered and shut down. Some children can not cope with scary, unknown emotions; they are simply not mature enough to understand. A sense of uneasiness and anxiety can occur from them taking it all in, even at a young age. For some children, despite the age when this could arise, they become cautious and careful as if they were walking through life on a minefield, watching their every step and waiting for the next bomb to go off.

At the age of nine, I experienced this emotional poison being thrust upon me by some of the adults in my life. The one that impacted me the most was my grandmother, whom I called a nanny. She was my mom's mother and had lived with us since I was two years old. Vividly I can still remember my grandmother saying to me repeatedly, "You will never be as good as your mother – she is perfect." Hearing her voice repeat those words was like a knife lodged in my heart, twisting deeper inside only to leave me feeling emotionally frozen every time she said it. This made it hard for me to look at Mom without feeling inadequate, assuming she probably agreed with the nanny. There was an image to be held, and being "the good girl" was my priority. Letting the family down or expressing feelings wasn't an option, and talking about my emotions was unheard of or dismissed as if I was crazy. Casual conversation was ok, but when it got serious or heavy, you did get to express yourself, and if you did, it fell on deaf ears or turned into a sarcastic debate. So I learned what I had to say was unimportant, which led to me withdrawing most of the time. My mom and dad weren't terrible parents; quite the opposite. They are great parents, and we always had fun together while taking family vacations and road trips and participating in plenty of game nights. Religion was an important part of our family; we were always going to church every Sunday and attending weeknight events. Dad and I went hunting and hung out watching TV, and sometimes I would go to work with him, and we enjoyed each other's company. It was harder for Mom and I to connect and do things. We didn't really have the same interests, and she stayed busy most of the time, but when we could, it was good. After working long hours, she would come home and tend to the nanny's needs first, and if, after that, she had any energy left for Dad and me, we would be able to spend some time with her. Most days, that time didn't happen because she was too exhausted for anything else, even herself. This was hard for Dad and me because we loved her and wanted to spend time with her, but we tried not to resent her for the exhaustion and how it affected us and did our best to be understanding. She is an incredible woman who I love dearly, all I wanted was her time. She did an amazing job at her work, and people loved her and were always excited to be in her presence. She would bend over backward to make life easier for anyone who crossed her path and would go out of her way to make others happy. Truth be told, I was jealous of her and craved her time and attention so badly. Especially, when I saw the way others enjoyed time with her; As many times, the nanny would tell me, "I needed to be more like my mom and needed to be better." It created a need to push myself to be just as good as Mom, if not better so that I could get the attention she did. Between the hurtful words of "never being enough" from the nanny and my mom's avoidance of me, I started believing that I wasn't worthy enough of anyone's love. Now, my dad's mom never spoke words that belittled me; you just had to proceed with caution when you visited her. She had a mean streak one minute and could be sweet the next. She was very conniving and loved stirring up drama only to lead to conflict between family members. Her influence taught me to be careful who I trusted. The grandmother I treasured and hated to leave when we visited her was my great-grandmother. Unfortunately, I didn't get to spend a lot of time with her. She could have been Mother Therese's sister. She was a sweet and caring woman, but her son was nothing like her. He was extremely mean and never treated her with any respect. I admired how she stayed strong and never let his nasty behavior change her disposition. She wore a smile like expense jewelry shines, had a loving attitude, and always had kind words to say, even up until her very last days. Her visits made you feel good, special and happy to be alive. At an early age we are dependent on the adults in our lives to provide food, shelter and love to feel safe and secure. As with any family, we all have those good and bad influences that form our emotional development. Surrounded by a variety of family members, I was never fully connected with any of them which unfortunately showed up later in my life through relationships. Trusting anyone to feel close was incredibly difficult with just about every relationship I had. Watching the adults in life scurry around, always taking care of the needs of others at the expense of the family or their own needs, I learned that to find your own happiness, you need to make others happy first. From their behaviors, I realized that working hard is what will always come first before family because it's important and necessary to survive and contributes to your happiness and well-being. The rules that I inherited were to never speak unless spoken to and always behave properly in public; otherwise, you would bring disgrace to the family.

As teenage years did creep in, sometimes getting punished was only about getting some attention rather than being ignored. Desperate to gain my mom's love and attention, I decided to show up as the daughter and image that she and her nanny wanted to see. I was hopeful things would get better, and they would be pleased with me. Putting on the mask every day over my true self didn't seem to change the circumstances, but they did seem happier with me. This charade lasted for a few years, only to leave me still unhappy with myself and even lonelier. Those weren't their expectations of me; those were mine due to all of the negative emotions swirling around in my head. They were raising me how they were raised and doing the best they knew how. Their domestication became my domestication. The problem was our relationships never developed well enough for them to see what was really happening to me or how I felt, which was mainly my fault for not sharing or expressing myself. I never felt comfortable enough to open up because I just knew what I had to say would seem like nonsense to them. It was hard to get close to someone who stays busy and is emotionally unavailable. Being emotionally unavailable means not being present, not responding to others' feelings, or being unable to share your own emotions. At the time, I couldn't see that part, but knowing what I know now, I wish I had spoken up and shared my feelings regardless of the outcome. I just didn't want to be a burden or a problem they had to deal with.

<u>Thoughts for Ashley:</u>

"Never let a child feel – Unseen, Unheard, Unwanted, or Unloved. At an early age, you are building your self-worth, self-esteem, and self-confidence. Remember – If we do not take the time to teach the world to our children the world will teach them for us, especially at a young age."

Love Mom

CHAPTER TWO

The Beginning of My Nightmares

"Trauma is a fact of life. It does not, however, have to be a life sentence."

Peter A. Levine

Dreams during this part of my life had been simple and enjoyable until one night, they shifted to ongoing nightmares. As I slept one night, this is what I dreamed; I was lying bare bottom on the crisp white sandy beach, patiently waiting for the magnificent golden sun to rise and the hot radiant heat to cover my body. Calmly, I embodied God's love and glorious hands surrounded me with a warm tenderness. Observing the calm, still ocean gently brushing against the shore, I felt the mist coming off the gentle waves. Closing my eyes to embrace the moment, I awoke abruptly, feeling heavy drops hitting my forehead. As I opened my eyes, the shadow of a man was standing over me, alert, I jumped up only to see darkness where there had once been light. Blinking a few times, I realized I was sitting in the middle of a marshy area that was dark, wet and dreary. Slowly standing up, I began looking around; I was taken aback by all of the sounds. It was heavily raining with a roaring thunderstorm crashing around the sky, while in the background there were several eerie animal screams piercing through the winds. In the distance, there was a flickering light; confused by my surroundings, my impulse was to move towards the light. As I began running down the narrow path through the bushes, several spiders and large bugs fell down from the tall trees that covered the path. Finally getting close to the opening, I was met by a badger pacing back and forth, daring me to cross. As he growled and swatted at me, I leaped over him and made my way to the building with the flickering light. As I slowly approached, a deep voice spoke to me. His words were, "Speak to me; it's not your fault." Chills ran down my spine as I opened the door. Naked and ashamed, I grabbed what looked like a pile of rags on the floor and immediately covered my body. It was a church; hesitantly, I made my way to the altar where I knelt down on the steps and began to pray. Wiping away my tears, I looked up; flashes of faces appeared in front of me, and loud, harsh voices began to speak to me. All of the people that had wronged me were now in front of me, scared, I closed my eyes, and the tears flooded down my face. Suddenly, I awoke, unsettled by these emotions from the nightmare. My body became engulfed and consumed by anger, sadness, and fear. This nightmare reoccurred for days until I finally understood. On some afternoons after school, I would stay at one of our neighbor's houses until my parents got home from work. For a few months, things went just fine until one day, the man in the home got too friendly. Expressing my discomfort to his wife, all I got was he was a little off, but he didn't mean any harm. Then, one day, things went too far; he did things to me that never should have been done. Assuming no one would believe me, especially when he threatened me not to tell, I never said a word.

More days like that followed, and my voice and body became numb to the events happening to me. Nervous and afraid to tell anyone, I kept it to myself. After countless afternoons of trying to fight him off, I began to hide in a closet until my parents came. Once I was in the closet, he would leave me alone. No one questioned it, and I felt safe. Never mentioning what had happened, I asked my parents to stop letting me stay there. They were confused and assumed I was just being a difficult teenager. I can't blame them; I never shared what happened. I was too embarrassed, and I knew they would think I was lying. Lying was a part of my life when I was young. Considering my pattern, how could I expect anyone to believe me? It was a way to cover up my true feelings and a desperate attempt to gain approval or attention from anyone who would listen to me. Quickly I realized just keeping the truth inside instead of lying about it was a better way to handle situations, or so it seemed at the time. During this period of my life, my friends grew, and friendships began developing. Even though I interacted with my friends, my need to spend more time with my mom never changed. We were like two ships passing in the days and nights. When she did stop from her busy life, she would pass out from exhaustion for days. When she was available or wanted to spend time, I already had plans. This would make her sad and depressed; I remember my dad always telling me to apologize for not being available or to simply cheer her up. I never understood why I was apologizing for something when I hadn't done anything wrong to apologize for. It helped her feel better in the moment, but unfortunately, that act carried with me my entire life. I was prompted to say "I am sorry." to anyone who needed cheering up, which resulted in me feeling guilty as if I had played a part in why they were depressed.

This stemmed back to the belief of always making others happy. Their depression or sadness would trigger my fight or flight mode; then I was left not knowing what to do, only to become emotionally frozen. The whole dynamics would change for me in how I interacted with people, just like the young and older children in the sandbox when hit with someone else's poison. Later in life, I learned this was being emotionally dis-regulated. Emotional deregulation can mean you have an underlying trauma that gets activated or triggered by a person or event. Little did anyone know that for a few years, I had been very close to suicide because I felt like I didn't genuinely matter to anyone. Starting high school, I encountered a few more sexual assaults that thankfully did not go as far as my first, due to my friends being at the right place at the right time. They might have stopped the nasty incidents, but they couldn't stop my nightmares. All this stuff kept happening and piling up, with no outlet or a way to release my feelings. Screaming on the inside only to feel numb on the outside. I wrote long poems, drew dark pictures reflecting my nightmares, and songs proving my unworthiness to live. During this time, being scared and lonely was my norm, but to the world, I managed to act like all was good. As Christians, we believe in God. He is what saved me from never following through with my suicide attempts. The times I came close to ending it, I would realize that disappointing God would be the ultimate sin. Striving to be perfect, I never followed through with any of my attempts. Passing this point, my dreams streamed back into better visions and messages, at least for a little while.

Dreams and nightmares are emotions, thoughts, feelings, and ideas that we involuntarily process in our sleep and sometimes during the day. The purpose they serve is to allow our brain to process our emotions and experiences. REM is rapid eye movement. During REM sleep, our bodies turn down adrenal, which is what turns on your flight, fight, or freeze when you're awake. REM sleep takes the intense feeling out of the situation you are going through and helps you process it better. REM sleep doesn't work for people who have PTSD because the adrenal can't shut off for them. Nightmares tend to repeat over and over again, craving to be resolved or healed. With PTSD, they can't get resolved because the brain has a harder time finishing it out to come to a solution, which causes repetitiveness and torment. Pondering the question: do dreams have meaning? Do they give directions, warnings, or tell us about the future? Some people live by what they interpret from their dreams. Some delight in the fantasies. While others can be tormented by what is called nightmares. As for me, I believe that my dreams and nightmares are God's way of speaking to me. Figuring out how to process a dream or nightmare all the way through to find a resolution can be done. Experiencing PTSD myself later in life has been eye-opening and difficult to overcome, especially when it comes to my nightmares. There are 3 types of dreams lucid, daydreams, and nightmares. Lucid is when you are aware or slightly awake and can jump in and out of the dream. It is like jumping on and off of a merry-go-round in sleep. I had those often; I could half wake up and realize I was dreaming but wanted to finish the dream, then close my eyes and finish it in my sleep. Good or bad dreams always affect me in one way or another. Not every night would I dream, but once I did see images and messages in my sleep, usually the next morning, I was eager to understand them. My curiosity would drive me insane until I got to the core of them. Most of the time, I can figure them out immediately, but some have taken longer to fully understand. Some have reoccurred over the years by taking on different meanings to either learn different life lessons or finally get the one it was trying to show me. Have you ever read a book several times, only to discover something new each time you reread it? My dreams/nightmares developed over my life and always showed up when I needed them, then stayed until I got the message.

Despite getting answers from God and understanding some of my nightmares better. I was still left with little explanation of life or an understanding at this age, so I sought after the outside world to get answers, only to be more confused most of the time. It wasn't until my sophomore year when I was working my third job, did things change for me. I met a woman at work who changed my outlook on life and helped me to navigate through it. We developed a friendship that has lasted a lifetime. This woman has a special place in my life to this day. Life got a little easier to cope with, and by seeing a different perspective I began understanding more of what I wanted and desired in my life. She taught me gratitude and a work ethic I hold true to date. Jealousy quickly set in with my mom over my new friend. The more time we spent together, the less I was available for time with her. Things became a little more difficult when I stopped asking her to do things with me and quit waiting around for her to do things together. Assuming I was acting out from being a teenager, nothing got addressed or discussed. So, my focus turned more toward working more and finishing high school, and soon, my life seemed to start to come together.

Fast forwarding to when I turned 21 years old, I got married and moved out and we rented for a year then decided to buy a house 45 minutes out of town. Shortly afterward, my grandmother passed away, and my parent's household changed; there was no grandmother to take care of and no daughter to keep up with. This turned my mom's world upside down, and empty nest syndrome set in. Suddenly, she had more time to spend with me. Figures I thought to myself, "Now you have the time to spend time with me after I have moved on with my life and busier than ever." Confused and bewildered, we managed to do a few things together. Trying to fit time into our new lives now had become harder, not to mention awkward. So, as time passed, the plans dwindled down to nothing, and life went on, having only a few conversations here and there. We became comfortable where our relationship was, and both seemed content or so it seemed.

<u>Thoughts for Ashley:</u>

Time is the most valuable gift you can give someone. Never miss an opportunity to spend time with your children. Have an open door policy we your children and make sure you have an open mind when listening. Because life can change in a blink of an eye, go to bed knowing you spent the day wisely – we only have one today.

Love Mom

CHAPTER THREE

They Will Always Be With Me

"It's (a miscarriage) all very thief-in-the-night. No one really knows what to say. You go into the emergency room, you think you're going to be a mom and you walk out empty. It's all neat and tidy, there's this potential being in your life and you're empty – all cleaned up and put back together, but completely shattered."

Tori Amos

After being married for a few years, I became pregnant, but I lost the baby within a few weeks. In a few months, I was pregnant again, only to lose one after another. I tried to stay busy and not face the heartache of not staying pregnant. My dreams and emotions would flood in and out, as I felt not good enough to carry a child. Fighting the words of my dreams, as they taunted me about not being good or worthy enough, I became pregnant again, praying and hoping for a full-term pregnancy. This one seemed to be settling in to stay with me. So planning our future was our next step. After making a trip to the Midwest to visit my husband's sister, we stumbled upon a new job opportunity for him. It was a caretaker position on a chicken farm, raising the chickens, which required us to move to Missouri. At first, I wasn't thrilled; I'm a Floridian and hated the cold, not to mention I hated birds of any kind during those years.

Having mixed feelings about moving and being pregnant, I wasn't convinced to go. Until my mom and I had a heated argument about moving with the baby, and we said some hurtful things that upset both of us so much; I called my husband and said let's move, my fight and flight mode had kicked in. Being pregnant, you are already so hormonal, and any kind of stress can flip your switch, good or bad. I was not a person who could regulate her emotions during this time in my life. I wanted to run as far away from her as I could because her pain was causing my pain and possibly my baby's pain, and I couldn't figure out how to help her or myself be better. I wanted harmony and peace in our relationship before I moved, but it just wasn't going to happen. I was stuck between resolving my relationship with my mom, getting to Missouri to help my husband, and taking care of myself and the baby, all of which broke my heart and crushed my soul. Without little ability and barely the strength to pack through all of this turmoil, my body started shutting down and feeling very strange. Giving into the rest that I desperately needed at that moment, I couldn't even manage to get settled into bed before passing out. That night my nightmares jolted me around like the winds in a tornado throwing around structures. It was like watching the news on multiple different channels with horrific displays on each one. I could see myself floating in the ocean surrounded by bottles bobbing up and down, with sharks circling me, ready to feast. Trying to reach and grab a bottle while the sharks rushed towards me, they started to chew off parts of my body with one quick attack after another. The ocean was filled with bottles, blood, and body parts; soon, reoccurring dreams appeared flashing one by one. I saw the little girl walking side by side with the elephant down the beach. As they passed the boxes on the beach, some were closed, and others were oozing with blood gushing out from all sides. Noticing the blood dripping out of the boxes onto the white sand, messages began to form. Looking closer, one message said, "Speak to me; it's not your fault." The next one said, "Find me before it's too late." As soon as I read them, my attention shifted to the sky, where a helicopter was spinning out of control. Watching the pieces fly off in several different directions, and then suddenly, it blew up. Pieces and parts were scattered all over the water; the faces of the people in my life were holding these pieces and parts.

Upset at what I saw, I glanced away, taking my attention back to the boxes on the beach. Opening one of the closed boxes, I fell to my knees and cried at what I saw; it was a lifeless fetus. Waking up sobbing from disappointment, here was proof that I had failed once again. Abandonment and rejection filled my head, while my self-confidence took a deep dive into remorse and shame. Struggling with the fear of loss once again, worry and doubt filled my body, awaiting life's next move for me. Laying in bed, reflecting on what I had seen, my choice to run away and escape from reality seemed inevitable.

The job required him to move first and I was to follow a few months later. While I stayed behind taking care of myself and the baby, Mom was still mad over my decision to move and voiced it every opportunity she had a chance. The stress and tension between us was really starting to affect me. Concerned about the baby I went to the doctor to have a check-up concerned before my travel was about to take place. Something wasn't feeling right inside, especially after the terrible nightmares the night before. Obviously, I was right; he quickly admitted me to the hospital. Being in my third trimester, I would talk to her daily, and this time, when there was no longer movement in response, I knew something was wrong. Reluctantly, I had to call my parents along with my husband to let them know I had lost the baby. Losing her would be a deeper loss than the other babies before; we had bonded through months as she grew, and now she could be gone. The drive to the hospital to finalize this feeling was extremely difficult, especially since we were also under a hurricane watch that day. While others were driving out of town, avoiding the hurricane that was about to happen, I was driving toward the eye of the storm right to the place where Ashley and I would part ways. I was not sure what I was dreading more, the separation from Ashley or facing the terrible emotions I would feel with life without her. Approaching the front of the hospital, I felt very overwhelmed; the winds had picked up to 60 MPH, and the emergency crew rushed me inside to a safe place. Questions upon questions were asked about preceding or waiting to have the procedure. By this point, I had bled out so much that my face was pale in color, and my speech was slurred. My clothes were covered with blood as if I was a person who had been mutilated in a "Saw" movie. The degree of pain from the miscarriage felt like I was passing a blood clot the size of a large orange through my body. Screaming, "Hurricane or not, help me get relief!" They rushed me back and began the procedure. Awakening from the aftermath of my D&C and the hurricane that passed through, all I could see were flashes of my mom huff-erring over me. Still feeling the effects of the anesthesia trailing around, my eyes would open and shut slowly, trying to pay attention to my surroundings. Eventually, I became fully awake only to hear my mom say, "All went well, and it is done." Crying over my loss, I began to shut down mentally to any conversation.

In the days to come, it was time for me to head to Missouri. With postpartum depression setting in, it was going to be an awful trip. Upon arrival, things seemed tougher than I expected. After leaving a place where the ones I loved didn't show they cared about me or supported me, and their only concern was about what they were losing, it seemed only logical I would end up in a place where it just continued in a different way. My emotional state had me convinced I was getting what I deserved. My loss and grief that inhabited my mind were quickly replaced with a lack of control and was draining my soul. That had been my life, trying to please others to gain my own happiness, only to feel worse and defeated. Tired, depressed, and not seeing my husband for a month, I was shocked when his only focus was on the day ahead. Frustration pierced through my hurt eyes, thinking to myself, when will someone care and take care of me? Forget that your wife just drove a 13-hour trip straight through four states with no stops, just had a miscarriage a few days ago, left with only postpartum depression, and was still hurting from the procedure because insurance wouldn't pay for pain medicine afterward; but sure, I don't mind sleeping on the floor. I was an emotional train wreck, and there wasn't a ticket for anyone else to board. For a few months, I stayed busy and fought my depression and self-loathing silently. Sweeping all of my emotions under a rug and feeling sorrow for myself could not be an option anymore. Ignoring my feelings, I decided not to stay mad and gave in to love, support, and help my husband instead of sharing the hurt emotions I was experiencing. Neglecting my health and my emotional state of mind had been a common occurrence in my life. Putting others' needs before my own was my belief, make them happy and they'll make you happy. Having multiple miscarriages by this point left me with an empty void and feelings of the many failures in my life. I had lost my patience and faith and forgot to rely on God's strength and guidance to get me through my father's needs before my own was my belief: make them happy in difficult times. Falling back into old habits, anxiety, fear, and worry made their way back into my head. Trying not to accept the notion that I'll never be enough was difficult to shake every day. Losing so much control by this point had me lost and confused. Instead of seeking professional help or guidance to help me cope with all my emotional baggage, I carried on with life as if nothing had happened. This was one of the biggest mistakes I had made in my life. It wasn't until later in life that I learned that you do only what you know to do at the time, and until you learn better, it was the best you could have done and forgive yourself. You can't do better when you don't know better, and I didn't know better. So, at this stage in my life, this was all I knew to do: set aside my feelings, work hard, and never look back. Pushing myself to get better physically and mentally was my new goal. Feeling the cold dark space I had stuck myself in needed to come to an end. My demons needed to find a new home to destroy.

After a couple of months, he made it known that he wasn't fully satisfied with this part of the job which led to changing jobs within the industry. He wanted to work as a boiler technician through the company. Just about every 6 months, he would express his unhappiness and we would change jobs again. We moved back and forth about every six months from Florida to Missouri and back to Missouri to Florida and sometimes to different farms in other states. This went on for many years. Life had become a monotonous cycle that was draining us mentally and especially financially. We would unpack only to re-pack a few months later when he would discuss his unhappiness again.

Struggling to make him happy hoping eventually he would return the favor and make me happy was a daunting job, and hard to realize it was never going to happen. Making others happy or their lives easier doesn't work for anyone, you are the only one who can make yourself happy. Others can make you happier, but they can't be responsible for your happiness – that's your job. Unfortunately, it took me half my life to learn this lesson. Over the next 15 years of marriage and a few more miscarriages, God blessed us with a healthy boy. Having a child helped shift my focus to our child and away from moving again. Being a mother brought me so much happiness, it softened me enough to try to rekindle my relationship with my mother. This new addition to our family helped bring my mom and me closer together. All of our issues were addressed and apologies were made, and my hope was to see the light at the end of the tunnel for a new beginning in multiple ways. Time passes and I'm pregnant with another healthy boy. Overflowing with delight and extremely grateful to God for allowing me to have two beautiful boys, my heart was rejoicing. Despite our newest addition to the family, the need to move again didn't end. The only change this time was the need to live closer to family and pick a different company. This move took us to Tennessee, where I was hopeful it would be our last.

<u>Thoughts for Ashley:</u>

"In order to find true and meaningful love, you must first love yourself. Take time every day to love yourself, you are worth it. Love yourself so deeply so that others add to your cup not feel required to fill it up for you. You

cannot give to others what you don't have for yourself. When you are mad, scream. When you are sad, cry. When you are happy, laugh. When you are hurt, express it. Never let time pass without taking the time to heal; love can mend all wounds only if it can be embraced."

Love Mom

CHAPTER FOUR

The Cycle Gets Broken

"Every experience God gives us, every person He puts in our lives, is the perfect preparation for the future – that only He can see."

Carrie Ten Boozz

Look out -here comes the family of gypsy's coming through again. Being married 20 years and moving about as many years as we were married forced us to drag around pets, furniture, equipment, and ourselves back and forth between several states, and now the kids were in the mix. This might have been more of an adventure if we didn't always end up back in the same place doing the exact same thing in a matter of time, only to pack and unpack a U-Haul over and over again. Constantly deep cleaning before unpacking, then in less than a year, packing it all back up and deep cleaning before you left. For every trip, we would sell our belongings and valuable items just to make packing a little easier each time and to have the money to rent the U haul. Praying each time that this would be the final move, so just maybe we could start to replace items sold or lost and finally settle down this time. Succeeding to make the trip to Tennessee and finding a place to rent, we immediately began to settle in. He was loving his new job, and it seemed like a good place to raise a family. Surrounded by mountains, the scenery was beautiful, clean, and friendly. Over the next few years, I got two part time jobs as a server and was homeschooling the boys. At first homeschooling was introduced merely because the surrounding schools were becoming overly crowded and teachers couldn't give each student the correct amount of time needed, but then I thought it would be a good idea in case we moved again. Here, I was already preparing and making adjustments, assuming there would be another move in our future. By my accommodating future plans, I was frustrated with myself to no end; I had been conditioned by my own beliefs and thoughts to continue the cycle I hated so much. It was time to switch my focus onto other things besides moving, so work, and homeschooling was my new focus.

Homeschooling was common in this area, but new to me. Once realizing my son had ADD and teachers didn't have time to help him the way he needed to learn, I figured it would be very beneficial if I could teach him one-on-one. This greatly helped him get caught up in a way that was comfortable with his own learning style. Homeschooling was one of the hardest jobs I ever did, but the most rewarding. Learning more about ADD and ADHD helped me navigate great curriculums for both boys (since both of them were now diagnosed). I researched and learned how to spot it with the adults and children I associated with on a daily basis. Realizing they're both inherited, I could see it in my husband and myself. Children and adults share the same symptoms with ADD or ADHD but respond and react quite differently. What they have in common is rapid thoughts, speech, and mental activity, the constant need to be busy, scattered thinking, and an impulse to be highly distracted, which causes them to sometimes forget things or never pay attention. Children need structure and routine, as for the adults that would make them feel like being a prisoner in their own home. Some adults crave routine, while others run for freedom. Children need help navigating ways to cope with life until they are old enough and capable enough to know how to make life work for what their requirements would be to function in the world. Adults don't want to be told what to do, whereas children do and usually obey their parents.

They want to be guided by the adults in their lives; do that to adults, and you'll smother them, which will result in retreating or withdrawing. Being easily distracted while either interacting with others or doing an activity is very common, but the downside can give off the impression that the person is uninterested or doesn't care because they simply can't be in the moment. As a person who always lived in the moment, too much at times. I could be distracted at times, but rarely allowed the distraction to take me away from the activity at hand or the person with whom I was with. Because I would overanalyze these moments, I could always tell if a person was genuinely interested in what I had to say or what I was doing. When they weren't in the moment with me I took it personally and shut down. Now, I'm not blaming ADD or ADHD; having it just makes the sensitivity of the situation harder to understand if you don't understand why it happens. Since childhood, people in my life who would not give me their full attention or consideration which rubbed me wrong, but instead of getting upset, I just went along with whatever was happening. Only to feel hurt and resentful later. This passive-aggressive behavior was my "go-to" approach; it allowed me to never stir up conflict and to keep others happy while always feeling obligated to do anything and everything they wanted or needed, so I would feel safe, loved, and never abandoned. Due to my lack of addressing the root of the problem, situations would occur only to be misunderstood, which always led to making the same mistake. Since I never opened up and shared my true feelings on everything, how could I expect them to do or even know what I wanted or needed? Pretending to connect with his dreams for the future, I would never considered my own. I was in love with the idea of making his dreams come true for him and never considered or cared how this was blocking my future. Falling into the emotionally frozen state of mind for most of our marriage resulted in me never knowing my true authentic self. Living a life of uncertainty and constant change can be unsettling if you allow it, and was for me. I was blind to how this was affecting me internally since I was so used to going with the flow. If I allowed any bad emotions to affect me internally, my anxiety would kick in. Many of us never stop long enough to reveal the person inside or our true desires. Anxiety blocks love for yourself and others, and ultimately you feel unsafe and unloved. This would bring me back to the nanny's words, "You'll never be enough or be loved enough." With this defeating mantra hammering my head, every day was a struggle to lift it high and feel worthy enough to face each day. Awful, isn't it? This behavior cost me my dignity, self-respect, and my voice. It wasn't until years later that I learned to set boundaries, speak my truth no matter what, and never allow others' feelings to control mine, but in this period of my life, I didn't have a clue that I was sabotaging myself and my marriage.

After a year, neither one of us had been truly happy and content in the journeys we had been on. Both of us kept looking for the next big thing or what would fulfill us. Due to our lack of communication, neither of us truly knew how the other one felt. There is nothing worse than being married to someone and never truly knowing what they are truly feeling or for them to know your true feelings; we both were guilty of that. We just passed by each other as we interacted with life together, assuming we both were good with what was happening. Falling back into my old patterns, I sought out what I loved, staying busy. While it is great to have multiple things to keep me occupied, the best part was it kept my mind off the unhappiness I felt in my marriage. My first job was in the city, and the other one was on the lake. The lake restaurant was my favorite, being near the water the view reminded me of the beach, my happy place. Despite the direction our marriage was going, everything else seemed to be falling into place until he started to have an itch to work on a chicken farm again. Obviously, people from Missouri were calling with job offers, or he wouldn't be entertaining the idea. When the conversation came up for discussion, this time, I didn't fall into agreement. For the first time, I stated my true feelings. I was tired of moving around all the time, being unsettled not knowing how long we would stay at a place, and dragging the kids around was not for me anymore. Realizing I was finally happy where we lived changed my perspective and my outlook on life. So voicing my answer, I said "No" instead of "Yes" and stood behind it. Married for almost 22 years at this point, I had never disagreed or went against his decision to move at any time. The man always got what he wanted if it was within our grasp or ability. Sound familiar? I did what my mom did with my grandmother and others. The "bending over backward to give them what they wanted or needed" to make them happy.

The problem is when you do that, it is at the expense of my own happiness, they win, and you lose. Looks like I had been taught well because that had been what I had done my entire marriage. It took years for me to realize making him happy wasn't going to happen. You can't make others happy; it's their job to make themselves happy. I'm not taking all of the blame because he made it clear that owning his own farm was more important than anything else in life, and everyone knew it. My hope was that if it could just happen, it would make him a happier man, and things between us would get better. I am to blame for never voicing or expressing my feelings for them to be heard, but finally, being happy with what I was doing in my life pushed me to take a stand. Taking this stand gave me the courage to express myself better with my mom in hopes our relationship would improve, and it worked. We finally could start the relationship between us with love and respect for each other. Back at home, things weren't going that easy. When he realized how I felt, he withdrew and was very upset. Talk about a mood killer; this became a marriage killer.

Restless going to sleep that night, Ashley showed up, speaking through my re-occurring dream. As she began running down the beach, she looked back at me and said, "Speak your truth." Gazing up towards the sky as the clouds were whirling around me, whispers could be heard. They repeated two phrases over and over again, "You are strong enough." and "Let your voice be heard." Following her inside the house of mirrors, I became aware that every mirror was broken, with several sad images of the girl displayed on each one of them. Glancing from mirror to mirror, confusion settled in as I studied each expression. Taking a closer look as I touched each mirror, the reflections switched to my sad images. Suddenly the mirrors turned into vehicles rushing past me. With the flashing of green lights to my right and red lights flashing to my left, I was standing in the middle of the intersection, trying not to get hit by all of the chaos of vehicles honking and breaking from the uncertainty of when to stop or go. Panic immediately came over my body, and my heart began to race. Scared from the panic attack that was slowly developing into anxiety from my dream, I quickly got up and went to the boy's room. Once I could see my boys, my heart settled down, and I realized it was only a dream. They gave me the comfort I needed to feel at peace. Anytime I was upset, I knew wrapping my arms around them could instantly calm me down, and it did.

<u>Thoughts for Ashley:</u>

To be present in a room full of people actively busy, never knowing you there, can be the worst kind of loneliness for someone. Not everyone can embrace the noise and filter through it without feeling ignored, unseen, or validated for their presence. If you can embrace the room without taking it personally and know that you are all you need in your life and not have the need for others to complete you – then you are a winner in the game of life. The best gift you can give anyone and yourself is your time and full attention.

Love Mom

CHAPTER FIVE

New Beginnings

"New Beginnings are often disguised as painful endings."

Lao Tzu

That night the dreams began to flood back in with all their might. Replaying over and over again. Echos of her voice telling me, "Speak your truth," caused me to wake up with a migraine and my body full of anxiety the next morning. Having second thoughts about expressing my decision, I wrestled with myself the entire time, getting dressed for work. On the drive to work, I played my favorite song. This song might sound cheesy to you and will certainly date me but I don't care. For those of you who know it, you'll understand, and for the ones who have never heard it well, I decided to share it with you-

The song is "Here I Go Again" by Whitesnake:

"I don't know where I'm going,
But I sure know where I've been
Hanging on the promises in songs of yesterday
And I've made up my mind,
I ain't wasting no more time"

"Here I go again, here I go again
Though I keep searching for an answer
I never seem to find what I'm looking for
Oh, Lord, I pray you give me strength to carry on"

"Cause I know what it means
To walk the lonely street of dreams"

"Here I go again on my own
Going down the only road I've ever known
Like a drifter, I was born to walk alone,
And I've made up my mind
I ain't wasting no more time
I'm just another heart in need of rescue
Waiting on love's sweet charity
And I'm gonna hold on for the rest of my days"

"Here I go again, here I go again
Though I keep searching for an answer
I never seem to find what I'm looking for
Oh, Lord, I pray you give me strength to carry on"

Listening to this as I approached my last job, I began to feel a little stronger and more confident. Praying before my shift, I asked God to give me strength to make the right decision for my future and the boys. Walking in that day, I was a little more reserved than normal. The restaurant was busy as usual, which made for a great escape from my current reality. During my lunch breaks, I always tried to go outside to take in the view and allow nature to share its beauty with me. I worked through my lunch break that day. By the end of my shift, my avoidant behavior obviously set off alarm bells. A few coworkers asked if I was ok, and of course, my answer was "Yes." During all the years of moving and restarting a new job every 6 to 8 months, I never opened up or got close to anyone. What was the point? You probably would never see them again. There were never questions to answer or stories to share; it was easier and less embarrassing that way. I was the mystery person no one knew anything about, and most of the time, people around me came to their own conclusions about who I was or what my story was, which was very interesting at times to hear their gossip about me. That part of moving was hard for me sometimes since I'm not a quiet or shy person; having the feelings to share or stronghold to never make friends or have conversations was heart-wrenching for my personality most of the time. So even though I had been at this job longer than the ones over the past years, I was still hesitant to open up. Needless to say, these folks were easier to get close to than others had been. The owner and one server had remained at closing that night; their persuasiveness opened me up. As I began telling my story over the last 15 years, a part of me began to shake, realizing that this was the first time I had allowed myself to be so vulnerable. I might as well have been naked on stage giving a speech to the president in front of the entire world, with the amount of fear and judgment that was inside of me at that moment. After explaining to them about all our many moves and how my husband only cared about what he wanted to do, not what the family desired to do, and sharing how I have remained a silent partner in the marriage to avoid conflict, I had stemmed to this unwelcoming decision. The question came, "What do YOU WANT to do?" Waterfalls fell from my eyes, and I began to tremble; no one had ever asked me what I wanted to do, not even my husband. Sure, I gave thoughts and suggestions, but my opinion about moving constantly didn't matter. It was always assumed I would follow along with the plan. Desperately trying to hold back all of the emotions that obviously felt the need to rush out of me at that moment, I was compelled to pause and then quietly answer, "I'm tired of moving." They both simultaneously said, "Then don't move." As simple as they made it sound, I knew it would not be that easy. Not sure what to say next, I took a deep breath and started gathering my belongings to head home. As I began out the door, they both reached out, and both of them gave me a big hug. This made me cry again; feeling the connection with others who actually cared about me was a new feeling. As I drove home that night, my heart felt warm, full, and loved.

Over the next few weeks, there was no discussion of moving. My curiosity was getting the best of me, so I brought it up. He sternly replied, "I waited too long to give them an answer; they had to choose someone else." Surprised with nothing to say, I just walked away. Months passed by and we became more and more separate in our living arrangement. We lived like roommates, not as a married couple. People at work kept encouraging me to give it another chance or try something different to rekindle the spark. So I decided to give it all of my efforts, only to become disappointed once again. Feelings of discouragement filled my soul while divorce danced through my head. Divorce had crossed my mind several times in our married years but never as strongly as it did at this moment. Marriage is not a one-person job; it takes two to want to make it work. Depression was glooming in the air, as thoughts of not being enough again began to slowly creep back in. I couldn't bear to have another failure in my life. As predicted, another job offer to move was brought up for discussion again. I held my ground and said, "No." He was very determined not to accept my answer but wasn't sure what to say or do. Days and nights of heated conversations and debates filled our life as he tried desperately to convince me to go. I was happy with everything in my life but our marriage during this time. This led to a whole lot of confusing thoughts for me to sort through. After one of our biggest debates about moving one night, I asked him to tell me his reasons for moving; his answers bewildered me and left me squandering the idea.

Confused and scared to make the wrong choice, I decided to get my coworkers' opinion. By this point I had developed closer connections with my coworkers, so asking for help and guidance felt safe and comfortable to do. After much discussion at work that day, I was still on the fence. So I approached my boss as he was working on one of the blinds in the dining room. Expressing my dilemma, he closely listened. It was when I mentioned the possibility of moving that his demeanor changed. He turned to me, eyes full of passionate tears, and asked, "Why would you do that? " Interested in his emotional response, I replied with a sarcastic laugh, "I'm sorry you might lose me as a server, but I'm not that good or special." He stepped down off the chair. Then looked right into my eyes and intensely said "That's not why I don't want to lose you." At that point, all I could do was take a deep gulping breath and froze from astonishment by his words. We both turned away from each other noticing everyone in the dining room was staring at us. Quickly we scampered away. My head raced that night on my drive home. Exhausted from overthinking, I decided to call my dear friend to get some advice. Upon explaining all that had happened that day, she reminded me of the prayer I had been daily praying to God. My prayer was this: "Dear God, please help me to be the woman I need to be for myself, my children, and the man in my life. Help me find love again. Let me seek your direction and guidance on decisions that are in front of me. Allow me to hear the path in my life you desire me to take." Without a doubt, God was answering my prayer, but my vision was too foggy to see. My friend shared some wisdom, and with love, she spoke these words to me, "What if the man God wants for you isn't your husband and by not moving will point you in the direction of your true desires and needs? You are asking for God's help but not seeing what it is because it hasn't completely revealed itself to you yet. Follow your heart and let God guide you." Going to bed that night, I prayed for clarity and peace of mind. It was the best night's sleep I had embraced in years, no dreams, only the embrace of putting everything in God's hands.

In the wake of events that had taken place, work became a little awkward, not fully understanding my boss's reaction to our last conversation. At home, it was like coexisting with a person in an apartment on opposite sides of the house. We had become strangers in our marriage, ones with aggression and cold actions between us each day. Our unhappiness was bringing out the bad sides of us both. We came together peacefully for dinner with the kids, then went our separate ways afterward. The kids were growing up and none the wiser to the intense silence their dad and I had between us. We never fought or discussed any major decisions in front of them, so to them, it seemed like this was a normal marriage. Not having a clue about all that was actually missing or deteriorating away from our marriage, they remained happy, healthy, and fun-loving boys. My days with them were great, they were the best thing that made my life tolerable and worth living. They are what drove me to get up every morning. The boys are true gifts from God, that I treasure every day. To tear apart their perfect world would make me feel like a monster, but we were so unhappy in our marriage. It seemed like the more I tried the more it pushed us further apart. Realizing that I had fell out of love with their dad made the idea of divorce seem catastrophic to tell them. Whenever the concept of divorce would enter my mind, I immediately felt sinful for thinking about it. Being a Christian, I knew it was against God. How could I be close to God if I went against Him? For many years, I contemplated divorce, but the thought of my children living in a broken or torn-apart home convinced me to stay. Until one day, watching my oldest son behave disrespectfully toward me, just like his dad had started doing because of his lack of feelings toward me. He threw around words as if women's opinions did matter, being talked down upon and belittled; this sudden change in attitude quickly changed my mind. Them watching our actions between us in our relationship had taught them these ways. Then my thought was if I stayed and said nothing, the boys would think that our marriage was normal and that is how women should be treated. After my mind shifted, I developed a cold heart and was tired of living this way.

Due to our lack of love, respect, and resentment for life decisions we had made, we were no longer holding back feelings, and the boys were picking up on it. Being in an unhappy marriage takes a toll on everyone involved. Simultaneously we both began to spend more time working later at our jobs and less time at home. We had the tag-out system with the boys. I would be at home with them while he worked, and then he would be home with them while I worked. This system worked great for the boys, but we never had time to spend with each other or as a family, which didn't seem to be important anymore to either one of us. Once I started to speak my truth, my self-confidence started to grow, and then the need to love myself became my priority, which led to knowing my self-worth.

<u>Thoughts for Ashley:</u>

"You must love yourself enough to put yourself first before you can ever truly love another or create a beautiful relationship. If you can't be your true self in a relationship, then you are settling. Settling will lead to resentment, anger, and bitterness. You come first!"

Love Mom

CHAPTER SIX

My Cinderella Story

"When all you know is flight or fight, red flags and butterflies all feel the same"

Cindy Cherie

Things at both jobs had been going well. Working more expanded my personal connection with more people which led to allowing my personality to freely come out. At the lake restaurant, the awkwardness between my boss and I had faded. We expanded our conversations and grew as friends. As time went on, it was interesting just how much we had in common. Slowly I picked up more shifts at the lake restaurant and was making more money. My plan was to save enough money to get a divorce and then go from there. One night my conversation with my boss got very personal for us both. Stumbling upon the fact that we both were unhappy in our marriages and recognizing the similarities was uncanny, which shined a new light on our friendship. When conversations began, we found ourselves babbling on about our marriages and the awful state of nonexistence we were both living in, constantly sharing some of the same feelings. Not sure where this was going, but intrigued by him, I allowed myself to spend more time with him. It was nice to have someone to take an interest in my life and actually want to hear what I had to say. We respected the fact that we were both married and tried to have boundaries, even though the attraction between us kept growing. Until one night, I let my guard down. It had been a long and hard week, and my dreams came back, haunting me with my grandmother's voice screaming, "You'll never be enough for anyone!" My husband had been spending a lot of time at a certain farm where I was sure he was attracted to the lady who owned it, especially due to his behavior around me when he talked about her. My instincts were longing for love, and I could see him drifting away; after all, we had become friends, not lovers anymore. That night after closing, my boss walked me to my car, and as we spoke for a little bit, my desire became like an animal magnetism toward him. Suddenly I was lured in by his eyes as if they were calling me in to engage. Our body language was as if we were in high school again. He began flirting with me with a sense of attraction, which made us both nervous the closer we got to one another. With my heart beating rapidly and my body craving his touch, I reached up and kissed him passionately. As my lips melted into his, a rush of euphoria filled my body. Then quickly, I pulled away and apologized. What have I done? We are both married. Shame and guilt replaced my emotional bliss. I quickly got into my car, trying not to look back at him, but I yelled from my car window, "I'm really sorry. I shouldn't done that." and drove away. Distressed, I called my dear friend. Hearing the panic in my voice, she immediately initiated the conversation with, "Honey, what's wrong?" Stuttering, I launched right into what happened. Interjecting a few statements like, "Oh my God, I can't believe I did that" and "We are both married" along with "I'm a terrible person." She patiently waited for me to finish and calmly came back with, "You're not a terrible person. It was an innocent kiss." Meaning well, she tried to help me feel better about what had happened, but my feelings of guilt stayed in my mind that night.

I called in sick the next day and didn't go back to work there for about a week. So, embarrassed about what happened, I couldn't imagine seeing him after that. At home, I felt dirty and avoided my husband as if I had some kind of contagious disease. Succeeding to pull myself together, I eventually went back to work. Returning wasn't so bad until later that afternoon he and his wife showed up together. Forget worrying about the awkwardness between him and me; now I have to socialize with her after kissing her husband. Anxiety hit the pit of my stomach, just thinking how problematic this could be. Somehow, we all managed to go untethered, even though we crossed each other's paths all day and evening. After everyone left and we were alone, he approached me. Looking at him timidly and sensing his hesitation, we both said in unison, "The kiss was wonderful." We slowly smiled at each other and reached out for our hands. We both hadn't felt that kind of passion in years. Quietly, I said, "This is wrong. We are married." He replied, "I know, but how can we stop now?" Puzzled by his response, I answered, "How could we do that to our families?" His answer surprised me. "How can we deny our love for each other?" I was startled because I assumed that the next time we saw each other, it would be a quick "I'm sorry" and "Let's try to forget what happened." Instead, we were discussing how to make it work. My head was spinning out of control. I swiftly let go of his hand and said, "Goodbye." Once at home, I jumped into my tub with some candles burning and soothing salts bubbling, hoping to vanish my thoughts and try to relax.

Over the next four months, things escalated, but we still managed to work together, trying not to get caught flirting from time to time. My dreams at night were filled with images of this man and our passionate kiss. Some nights, I battled with the thought of being with him and tearing my family apart, while other nights, the mere image of being together ignited my desires so strong the intense feelings would rush over my body, filling me up ecstasy with anticipation to see him again. The constant battle was tearing me up inside. When we slowly felt comfortable to talk again, the first thing he wanted to share with me was why it took two months for him to hire me. Thinking back, I was curious and often wondered why he refused to hire me the day I applied for the job. With my curiosity peaked I pushed to have the answer. As he proceeded to explain, he simply stated, "I fell in love with you the moment I laid eyes on you." He went on to say, "I knew if I hired you, it would only make me want you more, but I really didn't think I stood a chance." As he continued to explain the last year we had been working together, he admitted to always trying to be in the same space and place I was in and persistently kept track of where I was in the dining room at all times. Blushing, I didn't know whether to be flattered or freaked out, knowing I had a stalker and never knew it. I have always thought of myself as a person who pays attention to details and never misses anything going on around me. This man was good – too good. I had no idea he felt this way the entire time I worked for him. Overwhelmed by this discovery, I walked away speechless. Due to my silence, we ended the conversation and went back to work. As the day progressed, we resumed our flirting, and our eye contact grew with intensity. Every day, my heart grew deeper in love with him. The more time we spent around each, the more, we couldn't stand to be apart. This indulgent love I was experiencing was intoxicating. A little time passed before we had another deep conversation. Still in shock over his first confession and knowing that this man was passionately in love with me, he now used every opportunity to express it. With each of his words and confessions he shared, he had me yearning for more of him.

One night, I had a nightmare that was gnarly and petrifying; the next morning, I woke up in a panic state with my body trembling and immersed in sweat. Trying to recount the events from the nightmare, I quickly slipped back into it, only to see his wife's head on top of every crocodile's body thrashing around in the ocean, desperately trying to reach me on the beach. The only difference was the little girl was me, and I was seeing her face; this traumatized my fantasy of being with him. I just knew this was a sign from God. Scared to go back to bed, I just laid there playing scenarios of what would happen if we got caught. Never going back to sleep for fear of seeing all of my horrific nightmares play out again, I immediately got dressed and shot out the door like a bullet flying out of a gun to work. Impatiently waiting for him to arrive, the need to speak to him was imperative. The moment we were alone, I pulled him in front of me, placed a hand on each side of his face, looked him square in the eyes, and said, "We can't continue to do this while we are both still married. I'll see you in 12 years when my kids are grown and gone." I kissed his cheek and walked away. He was devastated.

Going back to work the next day, I never made eye contact, and I continued to do my job as if he didn't exist. This lasted only a few days. He trapped me in a corner at work and told me he couldn't live without me. I melted into his arms and agreed. Our love was too strong to lose, and neither of us wanted to live without each other. We returned to flirting, having more conversations, and the texts between us increased. Sparks grew more intensely as our love for one another shined like a forbidden light that had been hidden and now was making an appearance. Neither of us had ever felt this way with another person, our connection was so powerful we couldn't be separated. Because we started to show our affection stronger than before, people started to pay attention this time. Our spouses watched our moods change as happiness entered our lives again. It was so noticeable that eventually, we got caught. Oh did all hell break loose when that happened, and so did my nightmares. Closing my eyes that night, seeing nothing but darkness. Walking through the sandy beach, you feel between your toes coldness, not warmth. The sky was gloomy, with eagles and hawks flying over the still waters. The elephant is trying to walk down the beach, but instead of fighting off bees, it is wasps swarming him. There were no beautiful butterflies for him to walk by, only dead flowers along with the scattered half-opened and half-closed boxes with blood oozing from them. Horrified, you look away to the opposite side of the beach. Catching a glimpse of thrashing in the water, you move toward it to get a better look. There was the little girl crying and staring at crocodiles fighting with each other in the water. As you draw near, she turns towards you and says, "Please find me before it is too late! Alarmed, you freeze, and black dust begins to swirl around you and carries it all away.

<u>Thoughts for Ashley:</u>

Divorce might be a sin in God's eye, as each person can evaluate that for themselves. I feel when two people stay in a loveless and unhappy marriage, it is a tragedy. When children are a part of the equation in the marriage, it teaches them the wrong things about love and marriage. Follow your heart and never change yourself for anyone; if they truly love you, they will love you just as you are.

Love Mom

CHAPTER SEVEN

My Great Awakening

"As with the butterfly, adversity is necessary to build character in people."

Joseph B. Wirthlin

His wife didn't turn into a crocodile, but she was definitely a crazed animal when she found out. The bubble we had created to protect our love had burst into a million pieces and was about to be devoured by angry people whose only mission was to destroy us and the union we had created. They came after us with a vengeance, and everything was about to change dramatically and fast. The people who once enjoyed being around us now couldn't stand the sight of us. I immediately quit the lake job, mainly because my husband told me to and because I was tired of my coworkers glaring at me with disgust. I began working more at my other job until my coworkers from the lake job started harassing me there. They insisted on bringing attention to what we had done to everyone I had contact with, and everywhere I went. Since there was a long history with him and his wife, the mere idea of him cheating seemed unheard of. Naturally, they defended her and protested against him. This group of people were relentless. They drove by my home, protesting and blaring statements while casting stones constantly. They were like angry badgers on a mission to make our lives miserable, and they were succeeding. She went into a manic state, which inflamed their behavior toward us even more; this meltdown had turned into a horror movie. She began destroying their property one minute; then telling us we were made for each other the next. Her Dr. Jekyll and Mr. Hyde flips were extreme and scary, not to mention unpredictable. Our love affair had turned into our worst nightmare. Meanwhile, on my side of the fence, my husband had me going to our preacher, asking for repentance. Talk about being mortified and embarrassed, but obviously, that was the plan. His side of the family became so angry at me; his sister and her daughters were the worst. They sent very nasty text messages and voicemails and even blasted me on social media. I was portrayed as the whore, jezebel, tramp, slut, harlot, and more. Every chance they got they capitalized on reaching out to me some way and grind me into the ground for what I did.

All of the stress and turmoil resulted in a tremendous amount of guilt, shame, and spiritual berating, which made my menstrual cycle explode. The mental and emotional stress shut me down, and I was hospitalized. I was diagnosed with menorrhagia and hematidrosis. In layman's terms, it meant that my body was going through an incredible amount of stress, which caused tiny blood vessels to rupture and result in excessive bleeding. Anemia set in, and several medical bags of various amounts of fluids were quickly pumped into my body to help with my recovery. I had lost an enormous amount of blood. I began to fade in and out as they continued to pump more into me, in my mind the bags kept changing into boxes oozing blood as I drifted in and out of consciousness as I fell into dream after dream. The words, "Please find me before it's too late!" kept spinning around in my head. The mirrors in the dream were reflections of me and my heartaches, stress, and discomfort. Soon I went through each and every miscarriage one by one, feeling the pain my body had experienced with them. I wept as I remembered each moment. Being so emotional at this time, every thought reflects my mistakes. Knowing I couldn't go back and change things, and some I didn't want to change, left me with an unsettling peace. Through all this discomfort, they eventually built back my strength so my body and mind could begin to relax.

It was then that reality had sunk in and the realization that my world had been altered that I knew my life couldn't continue this way. My health was more important than my circumstances. Upon returning home, he had become angry due to the effect of the situation and how it had been taking such a toll on my health and our family. This increased his need to address it with my new love, and his wife wanted to confront me as well. After many apologies and begging them not to approach the other person, the desire for confrontation finally subsided in them both. The boys were the hardest part of this equation for me to deal with. Their loving eyes would longingly look into mine and wonder how I could have done this to their dad. How do you explain to your children that you have fallen out of love with their dad? How do explain to your children you have fallen in love with someone else? How do you explain to them that their dad and I were not happy? How do you explain you haven't spoken up for yourself during the whole marriage? Being so young, I knew they could never truly understand until some time had passed. So, all I could do was console them, apologize to them, and reassure them it wasn't their fault.

After my husband and I had multiple disagreements, fights, and crying sessions, it eventually sunk in I was no longer in love with him. We decided to get a divorce. Since what took place shouldn't affect the boys, we decided to use the same lawyer to make the process more comfortable and simple for everyone. We agreed to split everything 50/50, including time and money, and only take the items that we came into the relationship with. Despite him still being in love with me, everything else seemed to be mutual. As for the other side, his wife wasn't as easy to convince to get a divorce. She kept switching back and forth. One minute, she would give us her blessing, wishing for us to have a good life together, then switch to enraged and possessive, swearing that she would never give him a divorce. She kept telling him, "You can still see her. We can all live together under the same roof, but you will need to continue taking care of me and our son." That was an insane proposal. This unearthing of our love had flipped her switch. Her true mental conditions were appearing in rapid cycles that were stressful to keep up with for all involved. My divorce became final, and I moved to an apartment. Having the kids part-time was an adjustment for both of us. Homeschooling was even more difficult on a part-time schedule. However, we made it work. Otherwise, being on my own was liberating. My newfound love would come over when the kids weren't there, and it was nice, except for the fact he was still married. Waiting for him to get his divorce was an excruciating process that lasted over a year. She was determined not to give it to him. She didn't want us together, nor did she want to lose him. The biggest hurdle was her accepting the fact that her son would have me as a stepmom. In her eyes, I had already taken her husband, and she didn't like the idea of her son being with me. This was such a big deal that when they finally got their divorce, it was written in the paperwork that I was only allowed 3 hours of time with his son a day along with it came a whole lot of stipulations and clauses to follow. It was planned out day by day with financial requests and certain days they could have (some together and alone) until their son turned 22 years old. It was like signing a contract with Hitler. She took him through the wringer to get a divorce, but obviously, I was worth it.

Life in the apartment with the boys was beginning to smooth out some as we settled into our new reality. Even though situations with my ex-husband still arose, I set in motion a new attitude. This new attitude came from the freedom to make my own choices, hear my own voice, and live in my own direction. Liberation consumed me, and the mere thought of finally being in control of my life was thrilling. At first, excitement filled my life, then knowing what to do with it left me confused. I had never been on my own to do whatever I wanted without answering someone. I still had responsibilities with my boys and my new love, but making my own decisions was new and a little scary. Even though I still worked and homeschooled, I had so much free time to get to know myself. Hesitantly discovering who I was and what I wanted to do was a little hard in the beginning, but turned out to be a lot of fun as I figured it out. Opening up to my likes and dislikes was eye-opening. I realized I had done so much for others and never insisted that my needs were met. Every meal I made was for their taste buds, not mine; every time I spent with someone, I was always concerned about what they wanted to do, not me; we went places where others wanted to go while I never got asked or considered. Now, with the boys, I didn't mind it because my life revolved around them, but toward the middle of our marriage, I had made everything about my ex and not me. Now, this was completely my fault; I never spoke up or even considered my feelings. Their feelings came first. I am a master at putting others' feelings before my own, which is not a good thing. That was the biggest draw to my newfound love; he put my needs, wants, and desires first. No one had ever done that, nor had I insisted that they did. Now I'm doing it for myself and seeing it through different lenses. How unfair it was for me to expect more when I did everything; there was nothing left for him to do. Obviously I had taken it to the extreme and forgot about myself, never balancing the scale. There are people that you have to make happy for situations to be good, such as your boss if you're seeking a raise. Knowing that your approach and demeanor will affect your outcome, but for it to be done in a way that reflects your true identity without expectations is the key to balance. You can't just stop people pleasing in a relationship for it to work because there is a certain amount of give and take for both to be happy.

Relationships are not one-sided, nor shouldn't you be a doormat. I created the doormat for myself and allowed everyone to walk all over it at their leisure. Blaming others is wrong; it's like putting a cake on the table and telling everyone to take as much as you want, only to get mad when there is nothing left for yourself. Having unrealistic expectations from people when they can't read my mind or know my feelings is unfair to think they are responsible for helping, fixing, or making me happy. I put these unbearable expectations on myself and others, which led to disappointments, anger, and resentment. I was not proud of this discovery, but glad to have recognized it now than to never have known. I couldn't allow the people in my life to show up for me because I did too much for them! Creating a new pattern would require balancing other people's needs and your own to create harmony for yourself and others. By having all of this "me time," I could finally reveal more of myself and the mistakes I had made over time and begin to correct my ways of living; this was not going to be easy.

Thoughts for Ashley:

"All relationships have their ups and downs, but the most important requirements are communication, compromise, compassion, and patience. In order to fully show up for the "special person" in your life, you owe it to them to know yourself inside and out and love yourself unconditionally. Learn the difference between conditional and unconditional love; you owe that to yourself and others."

Love Mom

CHAPTER EIGHT

My Second Chance at Love

"It's not the load that breaks you down, it's the way you carry it."

Lena Horne

My new found love was still waiting to get a divorce, but that didn't stop my Cinderella story from evolving, and we never stopped seeing each other. Despite the hell he was enduring with his wife, he continued to stay hyper-focused on me. Our infatuation with each other grew to enormous heights; every moment alone was full of passion and great adventures. He was overflowing with ideas of exciting things to do and had impeccable taste in restaurants. Considering he owned his own restaurant and was a talented chef, I looked forward to any meal he cooked for me. Coming home one night after a very long day at work, I called him and expressed how my body was so exhausted all I wanted to do was soak in a bubble bath for hours. In less than an hour, he showed up at my apartment and cooked me a delicious meal to nourish my body. The best part was he fed it to me while I soaked in the bathtub. That intimate moment ignites my heart every time I think about it. I was spoiled and loved every minute of it. From morning until night, if we were not together, we were communicating either through text or conversation over the phone that lasted for hours at a time. Our words were flowing out of our mouths as if we had waited a lifetime to share every intimate word with each other. Exchanging these private times with someone special was a beautiful and soul-stirring experience. Lavishing me with gifts, I was the center of his world. One of the most romantic gestures I received was a picture where he had drawn out in the sand the words, "I love you, Lori." His charming ways and affection made me feel like a queen as this unbelievable courtship went on for months. We spoke for hours on the phone, always listening to each other unload our past experiences minute by minute, then lift each other up to feel alive again. Never before had someone taken that much interest in me and paid that much attention to me. It wasn't just about the romance; it was about talking and sharing feelings about anything and everything each night, and that brought us closer together each night. Convinced more than ever that he was my soul mate, I knew I had found the love of my life. Knowing that this man loved me just the way I was, made me feel alive and free. Free to be me, free to express myself, and free to walk confidently through life loving who I was. For once, I felt like I was enough for someone and was deserving enough for love.

Despite living in heaven with me, he was still experiencing true hell with his wife when we were apart. The constant battle for a divorce was bringing out the nasty sides of them both. Thank God his son was young at the time and couldn't understand all that was happening around him. Her demands were crazy, and her game-playing had enhanced our annoyance with the situation. She was fighting tooth and nail for him not to leave by making a divorce from her impossible. We would joke and say, "He was my knight in not-so-shiny armor due to his battle scars from her, and if he could make it through to the other side, I could put him back together." Upon occasion, she would use her son as a pawn; this was her main tactic in getting what she wanted. Her phone calls came at any given time, and he would jump to answer, never knowing if it was something important about his son or not. After much unnecessary time wasted, he decided to give in to her requests. This was only to stop the torture, not because he agreed with her demands. I begged him to make sure it was what he wanted, but he was over it all and didn't care anymore. All he wanted was divorce from her and all of the constant berating to stop, so we could get on with our lives.

With his divorce final, we could move on with our lives. It's funny how surreal it felt when it was finalized. This process had taken almost two years to be handled. Unfortunately, it didn't take her out of our lives or my ex. We saw and dealt with them more after divorce than we did married, it's insane how that works. My ex-husband had been difficult to deal with after the divorce as well. He was playing the blame game with my children, making them feel sorry for him, which in turn made me look bad for being happy. Needless to say, we tried to deal with them in the best way possible, having our children's best interests in mind. Many times we felt like just running away from it all, but we knew we couldn't. Now that he was divorced this meant he could start coming around with the kids. This opened the doors to all of our kids getting to know one another. At first, this seemed like a good idea, but it turned out it wasn't probably the right time. Forgetting that their dad had been brainwashing them about me and the new man in my life, things weren't going to be that easy. One day we all met at the pool inside my apartment complex. As we all piled in, jealousy reared its ugly face. My sons got jealous over any amount I spent with him or his son in the pool. They were so upset they began acting out, to the point of being rude toward them both. At one point he stood still in the pool and allowed my son to repeatedly whale on him, letting him get his frustration out. As noble as this seemed, it was unacceptable to me, so I immediately yanked my boys out of the pool and expressed my disappointment. We all got out and left each other that afternoon very distraught. This, in turn, resulted in a verbal lash back from the boys about their true feelings with two new people in our lives. Embarrassed and upset, we both were concerned about our future if the kids couldn't accept him or the situation. This put a wedge between us, which slowed our fairytale life for a few days. Regrouping, we came back together with a plan of action to get the boys to come around. We couldn't let anything else get in the way of our future together. We made plans with all of us going places and sharing new adventures. Some days were harder to cope with, while others were great. As we all got to know each other, things began to come together. It was when our exes caught wind of the good days we had that they started filling their heads with nonsense, only for us to resolve their thoughts and combat the negativity to get things back on track every time. During this period of time, I just have to say it "They were huge pains in the butts." Wishing they would leave us alone and get on with their lives would have been greatly appreciated. As time went on and our lives were intertwined, my future family seemed to be coming together. Next on our agenda was marriage and how to get everyone on board.

During this time frame, my dreams became vibrant and alive. They were illustrating where I had been and where I was heading. Close your eyes and journey with me as I allow you to feel what they showed me. There is a cool, brisk breeze filling the evening air, forcing the ornamental trees, which are scattered around, to hold the hands of the vibrant leaves attached to them while the breeze takes them on a dance. As the woman observes the rippling effect from the ocean waves plunging into the rocks beside the shoreline, she feels a mist of water piercing her cheeks. Its fierce and brutal body of water has a lot to say if one can listen. Shifting her attention to the right, she sees a path of unusually shaped rocks, some half in the ocean and others staggered one by one onto a patch of land. Drawn to them, she pushes her way through the crashing ocean to get closer. Forging across the heavy waves, she falls, and the rush of the current begins to take her away. Looking above, she sees a beautiful eagle circling; watching him, she suddenly realizes she has been washed out into the ocean. Desperate to get back, she begins thrashing her arms, trying to paddle back with no progress. Exhausted from trying to fight the current, she feels defeated. As she slowly floats into the ocean, she sees a platform off in the distance. Blinking a few times making sure she could still see it, she starts making her way toward it. Finally reaching the platform, she frantically tears it apart. Managing to tear off the whole side, she makes a board to lay on. As the ocean begins to calm, so does she. Closing her eyes, she fell asleep while drifting into the ocean. Awaken by a loud horn, she realizes it is a huge boat next to her. As she scans the boat, a deep voice says, "Are you ok?" Distressed, she screams back, "Please help me!" The man lowers down a rope for her to grab. Once she had a hold of it, he pulled her in. Reaching the deck of the boat, she immediately embraced the man and thanked him. As he politely accepted her thanks, she noticed he was alone. The conversation begins with the two of them. When he realizes what she is trying to do, he tells a story about the lighthouse on an island near the rocks she had described. She begs him to take her there. Full of enthusiasm, she replies, "I must see it. Please take me there!" Mesmerized by her beauty and excitement, the man knew he couldn't refuse her. They began their journey. As she stood at the point of the deck awaiting the arrival, her only thoughts were of the mysteries the lighthouse must have buried inside. The man sneaks up from behind and whispers in her ear, "You are so beautiful." Under normal circumstances, she would have been offended by the stranger, but this man captivates her soul. For the rest of the ride, they both laid on deck staring up at the stars illuminating the dark sky; laughing and holding hands until they both had fallen asleep in each other's arms. A loud booming thud awoke the romantic night when the boat had hit the shoreline.

Waking up thrilled about their arrival, they both jumped up to see. There was a magnificent rectangle-shaped lighthouse in the center of the island. Full of eagerness to go inside it, she drags the man off the boat and scampers as fast as her feet can move across the rocks. Filled full of adrenaline, she never thought twice about crossing the rocks this time. Wore out from the race to get there, the man stops her dead in her tracks and says, "Stop, let me catch my breath." She replied, "Come on, I have been waiting for this my entire life." He smiled, then began to join her on the climb inside and up the stairs. When they made it to the top, he proudly kissed her. Then she placed her head through the window where the light was beaming out and screamed, "Finally, I can see the light in my future." They both lovely grabbed one another and perched their bodies in a deep romantic embrace. After this dream, I immediately prayed to God and thanked Him for allowing me to find the love of my life.

<u>Thoughts for Ashley:</u>

"We all make mistakes and have lessons we need to learn. The lessons will repeat over and over again until we are forced to learn them. In life, when we get a second chance, never squander it; embrace it, and give it all you got!"

Love Mom

CHAPTER NINE

Our Bombs and Battlefields

"A strong marriage rarely has two strong people at the same time. It is a husband and wife who take turns being strong for each other in the moments when the other feels weak"

Ashley Willis

It was time for us to get married. We ran off to Pensacola Beach with a few close family members and exchanged vows. The ceremony went off without any complications. Oddly enough, that part was easy and simple, but what was to come later was straight out of Alfred Hitchcock's movie. Our honeymoon was over before we had one; we were heading straight into full-on combat. Once arriving home, multiple circumstances and events were quickly filling our lives, and none were pleasant. Things materialized like unwanted trash filling up a dump truck with nowhere to empty it. We were getting hit left and right with bombs from people and situations that were so intense we forgot we were a newly married couple and began acting like war buddies fighting to defend our home and family.

Hit 1 - My stepson's mother had texted and called the entire trip, worried about him; it was his first adventure out of town without her and to the beach. At first, I wrote it off as an overprotective mom, knowing he was with me and she hated me more than anything. I assumed the calls would tamper off in time. Over the next few months, that wasn't the case; calls became more frequent and even late into the night. This disturbed the entire family. Our middle son was affected the most because he shared a room with him. So when the late-night calls happened, my stepson was always left crying and missing his mom. Some nights it took hours for him to wind down and relax enough to get to sleep. This produced an incredible amount of separation anxiety between them both. The calls weren't for just her son, she was talking to my husband as well. It was always about their son, how the divorce was affecting him, or how to get parental advice. The funny thing is my stepson was adjusting very well until she would put upsetting thoughts into his head. Remember domestication and emotionally contagious adults flooding a child's head from their own issues? Well, here it was in action. Her mood reflected his behavior, which in turn affected the rest of the family. This made nights hard to get rest and days full of anxiety waiting for what would spark the next shift in what came next. It was amazing how well all three boys got along as if they had been brothers from birth. All was good until she was heard from or talked about. Then everyone's mood changed. The insistent continual interruptions didn't cease, they grew rapidly and more intense as months went by. This led to fights between everyone in the family. Our patience was running thin.

Hit 2 - The next turn of events was unexpected and very sad. One of my husband's oldest and dearest friends was hospitalized with no hope of making it out alive. My husband and I spent hours with him, up until the day came when he would no longer be with us. This was devastating to my husband; not only was he our dear friend, but also our account manager for our business. Losing him as a friend was hard enough but not having an account manager left my husband lost financially. Soon after he passed, lawyers were contacting us to go over his will. This was where things got ugly. He had left my husband in charge of his estates, which turned into pure agony. He was the executor of the will along with a friend/lawyer who required his vote to finalize any decisions. For a man that seemed like he had money, it was quite the opposite. He was overextended and had properties scattered all over the place, all with unknown names of who occupied them. We became detectives with lawyers sucking us financially dry, figuring out the burdens that we inherited. We fought with lawyers, lost money, and the friend/lawyer that he had to make decisions with had screwed him over. We were left with debts to pay that weren't ours.

Hit 3 - At the same time, our business seemed to be profitable, but after looking over the books, that wasn't the case. Our friend who passed away left us with a huge mess. It appeared that as his health was declining, so was his accounting skills. All of our accounts were a jumbled, disorganized pile of numbers that didn't add up correctly. Trying to sort through all of it was very time-consuming. Once some headway was made, the realization of having no profit, no money, and more debt than we could handle, I became paralyzed with fear. Financial discussions were now at our forefront, and that didn't help a new marriage. At this point, our stress levels had increased, and anxiety filled our lives daily, which made work life harder to enjoy. Almost all of the staff that had been with him for years left after the divorce. Having to hire new staff turned into a constant revolving door of people coming and going, which in turn was difficult to constantly have to train new people daily. As busy as were and needed to be, it was very hard to keep up.

Hit 4 - Being six months into our marriage, with all of the turmoil that filled our home now, my husband and I drastically changed. For every turn we took, more and more stress continued to fill our lives, which immensely affected our work, home, and love life. I returned to old patterns of the over-functioning, over-giver, the codependent person I had tried to leave behind. He was slowly losing control of things, and rightfully so, due to the extreme amount of pressure he had been left with on his shoulders. He became easily agitated, mad, and angry, which was hard to live, but I understand why. Feeling like he had been handed a deck of bad cards, I jumped in to help him. Thinking at the time that it was the right choice, not realizing I was starting a nasty cycle with my new husband, I began putting others' feelings first and completely forgot myself. Every day we both were filled with crippling anxiety from all the stress that had been dumped in our lives, this led me to try to fix it and make him happy so we both could be happy. Being a positive person, assuming if I picked up the slack when he was too numb to cope, it would make the difference was my first mistake. Choosing to fix it and make him happy was my second mistake, and falling into old patterns that didn't work was my third mistake. Ultimately, all my mistakes and his out-of-control attitude drove a wedge between us. Roles shifted at work and home as I took on more jobs and responsibilities, trying to help out more. Forgetting my past, never did it cross my mind I was enabling him and not allowing him to be the man in the equation. Over time, the help was appreciated, then slowly changed to resentment, and avoidance crept in for us both. The more I enjoyed running the business, the more it made him mad and miserable. Managing a business was my dream, but I was unaware he felt like I was taking his dream away. That was never the intent; becoming a great team was my goal. Confused by my efforts to save my husband and the business, I slowly stopped helping and became quickly invisible. I went from running the show to hiding from it, as everything was unraveling.

Hit 5 - -Life wasn't any better on my ex's side either; the boys were living in a trailer about a mile from the house where he stayed with his new wife. She didn't like them and wanted nothing to do with them, and made it crystal clear to them both. This broke my heart, they were great kids and I hated that she couldn't see that. At this time, my oldest was 12 years old, and my middle son was 8 years old. Knowing they stayed alone in a trailer off a busy road at night scared the sh** out of me. Countless calls every night were made just to ensure their safety for my own peace of mind since there was nothing I could do about the situation. If I reported it, they would have to speak against their father which was clearly not going to happen. I was stuck at everyone's mercy; I had no choice.

Having no control sucks, especially when it comes to your children. The saddest part is that it is still the case 'to this day, not with my children but with life in general. I had become a high-functioning codependent and forgot all of the mistakes I thought I had learned from this. It frustrated me to know I was faced with them once again. I was rushing to fix everything, help anyone, and took on others' problems as if I didn't have enough of my own. I was the "fixer," "go-to person," "emotional dumpster," "the giver," and the "over-functioning person." All of this urgency led to exhaustion and resentment toward others who didn't give or help me back. I let them drain my cup without ever taking the time to fill my own as if it was their job to do. Doing more than your part will never fill your cup, and not allowing anyone to fill yours will never help the situation. Looking back, I feel foolish for stepping out of my lane and jumping into others, which quickly became my demise. With no balance or knowledge of what I was doing to myself, I ended up being a train wreck in action daily. What once was a beautiful new life and a promising future was now flipped upside down, casting dark clouds everywhere I turned, thanks to my own sabotage. My husband wouldn't speak to me, and my kids were scared to tell the truth for fear of what I might do with it or say about it, and the constant battle to stay financially secure was never-ending. Afraid to say or do the wrong thing, I was walking on eggshells constantly. Life was consuming me with all of its negative energy, and I had no idea what to do with it. Demons lingered in my head during the day and night. Every step I took, I felt like someone or something was choking the life out of me. Bewildered by my efforts, anxiety swirled my thoughts between not being good enough or the opposite extreme when I was too good at something or too helpful; people resented me. Knowing that if I talked to my husband about my feelings, it would only make him more stressed, I decided to reach out to a counselor for advice.

Fast forward a few years, and after many sessions with multiple counselors trying to reset my mindset, things slowly started to settle down and come together in our lives. My husband and I made some life changes and adjustments, which allowed home and work to get better. I backed off and tried to learn my own life lessons again while he worked on his. We learned to love each other's differences; he loved my light, and I loved his dark. After drudging through all the muck life had thrown at us and cleaning up after other people's contamination, our marriage was at the helm of being restored, even still having a few stressful moments from time to time. Our love grew stronger, despite our uncomfortable circumstances. My ex and his wife made a few alterations in their home life as well, which allowed the boys to live with them. That was an answer to prayer, no more sleepless nights worrying about their safety. His ex was leaving us alone, and things began taking an about turn in good direction, or so it appeared.

<u>Thoughts for Ashley:</u>

"While waiting for the storm to pass, admire the storm, then dance in the rain and sing praises to God for it all. Accept your mistakes and learn from them."

Love Mom

CHAPTER TEN

Beauty and the Beast

"Trauma comes back as a reaction, not a memory."

Bessel Van Der Kok

Call it the calm before the storm, which was exactly what happened next. All had been quiet and calm until one weekend; we were under a tornado watch; luckily, it never came in our direction. We had all of the boys with us, and we remained safe. Unfortunately, that night, it hit his ex-wife's house. Her entire surrounding area had major damage, which naturally sent her into a state of shock. Due to tornadoes' unpredictable nature and devastating destruction, it would take a while to bounce back from the physical damage, emotional distress, and post-traumatic stress one might been left with after such a terrible act from Mother Earth. Luckily, she and all of her family came out alive and with minimal damage to their home. The next day, we volunteered to help clean up; it was a somber day as we gathered all the debris and put things back together. It wasn't just the tornado's destruction that sent her into overwhelming anxiety; it was the aftermath when they were told to leave the home for repairs to get underway. We kept our stepson for a couple of weeks while she found a place to live and handled the process of moving everything from place to place. She lived with her parents, had multiple pets, and had lost some items in the storm, so this was going to take some time. She was not accustomed to handling this much responsibility. Up until their divorce, she was dependent on everyone in her life to handle situations and decisions for her. They prevented her from functioning as an individual to cope with real life, so this was going to be a difficult task for her to handle on her own. As the weeks went by she and her son talked more often due to the situation, we didn't mind because it was needed for them both. We helped her make decisions and talked to her many times to reassure her that her life would get in order soon. After a few weeks went by, it was finally time for her to get her son back. On the day before we were meeting with her to reunite them, something horrible happened.

Everyone in the house was about to be awakened that morning, not by a glorious sunrise but by a horror film taking place inside their home. We were all abruptly woke up to the unwelcome sounds of loud banging on our front door, followed by my deep demonic screams. It was his ex-wife; she was having a manic attack here at our home. Hearing her scream, "Give me my God damn son," sent him and me into a panic and sent chills down my spine. Franticly, I rushed down the stairs to get to all three boys for fear she might get to them first. As I started down the hall to each door dodging bits and pieces of broken glass scattered everywhere, all I could hear was more screaming and glass shattering. She was making her way around the house, breaking each window and throwing anything that she could get her hands on off the porch. I safely managed to get all three boys to the back of the house in a room with no windows and called the police. Meanwhile, he had raced downstairs and was watching her through our unbroken windows, trying to talk her down. Sadly this wasn't the first time he had experienced one of her manic attacks; several had taken place during their marriage. Having heard the details of each one from him, the images he shared with me sent my mind into a frightening state of fear. Explaining to the police about what was happening became incredibly difficult as my stepson was listening to every word I said. Here he was, staring at me, crying and asking, "Why is she doing this?" My heart was breaking for him. All three boys were either scared or confused. Waiting in that room for the police to arrive and put an end to this nightmare was grueling. We sat in silence, listening to glass breaking, screams from his mother, and his dad's loud voice trying to stop her, while in the background, you could hear loud gospel music blaring from her car, which was still running parked in our driveway. What seemed like an eternity finally ended with an officer's voice telling me it was safe to come out. It wasn't easy to convince me to open the door. It took some persuasion on his part, as we all were too frightened to move. Once coming out, I sent the boys to the closest safe room and told them to sit still. Hesitantly walking down the hall, I had to keep being reassured by the officer that it was ok. Until he said, "We have her handcuffed in our police car, which is parked right outside your front door," did I pick up the pace? Carefully walking into the living, avoiding glass on the floor and never looking out the front door, I saw my husband run to him and began crying while embracing him so tightly. After allowing us to have a few moments, the officers started asking us questions. After much explanation and conversation, they drove her away. After they left, we both went out onto the porch and stood there in shock, looking around. Everything we once had on the porch had now been destroyed; all my plants were ripped out and torn apart, three windows were broken, and mangled chairs and dismantled tables were tossed into the front yard. Our wooden rocking swing had been picked up and shoved to the other side of the porch, which weighed close to 200 lbs. (it took three of us to move it). The

43

adrenal and manic state that she was in had become so intense that it was as if she had superpowers. Gathering our senses and trying to make sense of what just happened, we made arrangements for the boys to stay somewhere else. Once they were taken care of, we obtained restraining orders against her to keep all of us safe. Then, it took days for us to get windows fixed, glass cleaned up, and the house somewhat back in order. When we all came back together, sleeping through the night was our next battle to conquer; it took a lot of night medicine and time for all of us to rest through the night normally again. Remembering the first night for myself was terrifying; when I closed my eyes, the images of her face and her voice haunted me, with the incident replaying over and over again. Clinging to my husband, I was shaking from fear and crying the entire night. For weeks, we woke up several nights to our stepson screaming and crying; he couldn't shake it either. My husband and I would jump at sounds that triggered us and my other two sons just tried to zone it all out.

Desperate for relief for us all, I knew we needed help. Explaining briefly over the phone that we had an urgent family crisis, our counselor gladly agreed to see us. So on the next morning's agenda was a trip to see him. As we all sat waiting for our turn to be seen, the amount of negative energy was so intense in the room no one made conversation or eye contact. Each one of us held our emotions in different ways. My curiosity about each person's view on the incident drove me crazy. I watched with much anticipation on everyone's faces as they left his office, hoping to see a sigh of relief instead of the emptiness that had been on display for weeks prior. I was hoping that the counselor would be able to pull it out of them, so their healing could begin. Then it was my turn. Since the counselor and I knew each other very well from past sessions, he expected I would be very concerned about everyone but myself. Through the past few years, we have developed a special friendship. I would help give him insight into each family member and exactly what they were experiencing in their life since none of them felt comfortable enough to open up with him. He had told me many times he thought that I was a caring, intelligent, loving person who always had the best interest of others at the core of my heart. He respected the amount of studying and research I had done to help him know exactly what they needed help with before they showed up for their session with him. He always appreciated the advice and told me I needed to seek a counseling degree of my own one day. So our session started with the question, "How are you doing after this traumatic event happened?" He went right to me and wanted no discussion about anyone else. Dancing around the question, I tried to talk about family members, but he wouldn't allow it. Stunned and becoming very agitated that he wouldn't let me talk about my family, I started to shut down. He finally said with a stern and deep voice, "This session will only be about you, your emotions and feelings concerning the incident, and how you are coping - nothing else!" Glaring at him, I became mad and angry. I screamed back, "WHY!" Then the tears rushed down my face, and the words rolled out as if the gates to my dam had been broken. "She violated all of us, took away our safety and security, our freedom to step out the front door, and she shut our whole family down, especially me. We became silent, avoidant, and numb to life in the days that followed. That morning she would have killed me if I was on that front porch. Every morning, I went out on the front porch before my family got up. I drank a cup of coffee and prayed to God for a good day. That morning was the first time in years I overslept to what became one of my many nightmares.

God saved me! I became scared of things I had never been scared of before. Some nights, the mere thought of her chasing after us in an attempt to kill all of us leaves me trembling so bad I lay there parallelized," I blared. Continuing to express my feelings as the walls that once were fiercely built around me came crumbling down. Out. The green light to store up emotions had rushed out before I could hit the stop button on them. Having been so bottled up, everything began to spew out like Mount Rushmore erupting - resentment, anger, bitterness, jealousy, depression, loneliness, abandonment, self-denial, unworthiness, acceptance, approval, and much more. As he helped to unravel my bare naked truth, a sense of easement developed. Reflecting back to her traumatic event with the tornado, compassion filled my heart, and sadness penetrated my thoughts. She went through a lot, and her volcano erupted as if her lava had poured over our life to burn and destroy anything in its path. She might have been to blame for the actions, but to blame her for her mental state didn't seem fair. A sudden shift happened; expressive words about the woman who caused the incident changed to the blaming and dissatisfaction of all of the people in my past who had caused so much pain. Story after story began to gush out, it was obvious that I had been carrying an extremely heavy load for over my whole life. Realizing that there was more to unravel and discuss, the counselor noticed that our time was about to run out. It was decided that future visits were needed. His assignment to me was, before their next visit, to write down in a journal the whole story of each person in my life that caused my pain and why for our next session. He wrapped up with this statement, "The loved ones in your life have always come before yourself; they enjoy and appreciate your love, devotion, and all the time you invest in them. Now it's time for you to do the same for yourself so you can reap the benefits of being loved by someone like yourself. You are an amazing mother, wife, and friend. I'm thrilled to know you. It's time for you to get to know yourself and see the beautiful person you are. Help heal yourself so you can continue to love yourself in the incredible way you do for others." Walking out of the office, I was dazed and mesmerized by his words. Feeling overwhelmed and locking eyes with my family, I noticed they were watching with anticipation for my reaction. Suddenly I felt guarded and locked down inside once again. With my heart racing and tightness building up in my chest, I turned all my focus onto the family. Once again trying to hide my true self to appear not broken, so I could be strong for others.

<u>Thoughts for Ashley:</u>

Learn to release all that doesn't serve you, never hold things that anger you, forgive others as God forgives us, and search for healing.

Love Mom

CHAPTER ELEVEN

Bark Street

"A lack of transparency results in distrust and a deep sense of insecurity"

David Richo

oming home that evening, we all sat in silence at the dinner table. No one was quite sure what to say, and all seemed lost in their thoughts. When everyone was done, they all buried themselves in some kind of distraction or device, trying to forget what had happened that day. Some were mad that we had gone to speak with the counselor, while others were trying to forget the whole thing and move on. As for me, I went upstairs, sat in bed, and pondered the counselor's last words to me; he had opened a place in my heart that had never been allowed to be touched. With a house full of people the sudden realization that I was completely alone in this journey, dread engulfed my body. As the counselor suggested, I decided to start a new journal. The words, emotions, and pain began to flood out onto my pages. A multitude of situations and mixed emotions that I had never revisited before began to shine, and the uprooted mental patterns that were being developed had caused me significant distress and anxiety, impairing my personal functioning and, at times, completely shutting down my brain. Reflecting back to my many conversations with my dear friend and multiple sessions with the counselor, I realized these two people were the only ones to truly know everything I had sacrificed for myself in an attempt to help others. Keeping others at bay about my true feelings would keep them from getting hurt or being misunderstood. I had always been there for everyone else but never for myself. Consideration for the needs of others came before mine. Hell, I didn't even know what my own needs were, much less how to get them. Toxic thoughts swirled around, chasing away my loving and non-judgmental headspace while simultaneously distorting my thoughts and stories. Suddenly, I was taken over by a victim mentality, which made me reach up to cover my heart to guard it tightly. Fighting the intense amount of rage that was filling up inside me, flashes of people in my past and present were triggering my nasty emotions. Irate at myself, I shifted the blame onto others for taking my help and never returning the favor. If they wanted it, I made it happen or did it. If there was an issue they were coping with or needed help with; I would research, learn about it, and discover ways to help them through books, internet, podcasts, and even counseling on my own or with them about their situations. I knew more about them and how to cope with their situations and conditions than they did. Over time, they would get better, while I would become emotionally drained and exhausted. They would keep taking the help, keep it as their own discovery, and carry on with their lives. Thank you never came and gratitude never showed up. Oddly enough, the people in my life never knew how I felt or the amount of stress I was carrying because I never expressed it. Due to my lack of complaining or expressing my feelings, changes in my attitude were the only sign something was wrong. I was once a positive person with a supportive personality, but now I have become a negative person and resentful one.

I didn't like who I was becoming. No one asked how I felt except my children. They noticed the change in my behavior and were concerned. My children were the exception; by helping them, I received joy and pleasure as a mom. Feeling anything but love and appreciation from them made me happy. As they grew in age and independence, they didn't seek as much help. When help or guidance was needed, I felt their unconditional love shine through every time. It was harder at times, but it never seemed like a burden to be a mom, and I know it never will. This act of love made our relationships very strong and unable to shake, which I am extremely proud of. Recognizing you have raised your children in a good way makes it important to listen when they share their worries and genuinely want to understand why you have suddenly changed. Embarrassing as it was to be called out by your kids, a feeling of delight quickly replaced the negative feedback, knowing all they wanted for me to be fully happy. Over the years, listening to them express their concerns made me self-conscious, knowing I wasn't practicing what I preached. In all of those years of giving advice, never once did I take my own. Looking back at all of the people I was blaming, it wasn't completely their fault.

As a woman who bluntly spoke her mind when she was passionate about something, I noticed these passions were being replaced by my pain and hurt as the words never came. The stress in my life had smothered me as if life was holding my head under water. Being passionate about myself wasn't happening, hence the silence. When the attention switched to me, shutting down was the easiest answer. What an idiot I had become, pointing fingers at others for my actions and reactions. No one held a gun to my head; it was my choice to be overly invested. Blinded by my own ignorance and desire to be loved and acknowledged for my efforts, my demons and monsters were being released. Not being fully honest with myself or with others only left me bitter and resentful, and it was time to stop this insane roller coaster of self-destruction. Now, being told by the counselor to put myself first and focus on myself, the confusion struck my head like a brick. It had been easy to help others because you knew exactly what they needed, but to help myself? I didn't know where to begin.

As I closed my journal, my body and mind slowly drifted to sleep. Falling deep into the darkness of the night, I was taken back to a small rural town surrounded by rolling hills and farmland as far as you could see. In the distance sat an old, dreary house; most assumed it was condemned and uninhabited. The house was dark, dingy, and structurally falling apart. It was consumed by overgrown trees; poison ivy covered the walls that separated it from the outside world. The gates that bordered the land were wrapped up with thorny bushes and rusty barbed wire left from fencing that had once embodied an active pasture field of cattle. The long driveway to get to the house was nestled deep into the estate and lined with silver maple trees. What once was a beautiful functioning cattle ranch was now a broken, run down unproductive piece of property. Realizing the land owner had passed away, rumors about the remaining family and the estate consumed the community. The locals had many of their own stories. Some would say it was haunted and abandoned and that squatters passed through coming and going from the home. Others swore there was a witch that lived there, and at night would step out on the porch to cast spells on the people of the town. The truth about the estate on Bark Street wasn't quite what the gossiping town had imagined. Living in this small mid-west town, boredom set in on a regular basis, so some afternoons, I would find myself driving by the dim-lit rickety house and parking off the road, wondering what the real story was. Often I would get a glimpse of someone peeking through the shredded curtains. As soon as the uncomfortable realization that someone was watching me watch them set in, I would quickly drive away. Visiting the local post office one day, I decided to ask the lady behind the counter about the house on Bark Street. She was in her late 80's. She and I had become friendly, and knowing that she knew everyone in town and their personal business seemed like the perfect idea. Once we were alone, I asked, "So, do you know the real truth about the house on Bark Street?' She carefully looked around, grabbed my hand, and then cautiously said, "Honey, you best not tell a soul if I tell you." Surprised and curious, I replied, "Your secret is safe with me." The woman who lives in the house is my 50-year-old daughter. She lives alone and never leaves the house. We've tried to get her to fix up the place after my husband died and sell it, but she was never ready to leave. The estate and property would sell for millions if some work was done. When my husband passed away ten years ago, she began fixing the inside to bring it back to its luster. This allowed her to be more comfortable living there, but the outside and foundation never received any attention. For a little while, hiring help for the inside of the house worked well; as soon as the outside work needed to be addressed, the work stopped immediately. Receiving help from others became excruciating for her. All improvements and work came to a halt, we she would become uncomfortable. Years passed, and she continuously stayed sick. I would stop in to drop off supplies and bring the doctor with me to check on her, but for every medication he prescribed, she refused to take. Eventually, she became depressed and showed signs of schizophrenia. After many visits from multiple doctors trying to help her, a final visit diagnosed her with agoraphobia. Once he explained, we both were shocked. At that point, I made him swear on his life never to tell another living being. My daughter has never left the house since, and no one except me ever goes inside with her. Agoraphobia is when a person develops an anxiety disorder that causes them to be afraid to leave the environment they consider safe. Waking up startled by the memory, something resonated with me. What had happened made me feel unsafe to leave my environment. I had lost my peace and was afraid; my body and mind changed drastically after the incident. Old and new thoughts rushed in as I tried to make sense of what to do next. Flooded by mixed emotions followed by excessive bleeding, anxiety engulfed my body. The heavy bleeding had resurfaced once again, this time with a vengeance. Forcing its way through, resulting in hours of changing clothes, passing large clots, and having severe menstrual cramps, an urgent need to go to the hospital appeared in my thoughts. Realizing I was home alone, panic set in. Dragging myself downstairs and into the car, I drove to the hospital. During the drive, I began to feel weaker and dizzy. Pulling under the ER breezeway, I motioned for help. Explaining my shortness of breath and tightness in my chest, they rushed me inside. This was all too familiar but more frightening than before due to the multiple anxiety attacks I was having. Nurses rushed in with fluids and started checking my vitals. Undergoing hours of sleep ended up being the best rest I had received in months. Hesitant to wake up and get back to reality, I was awoken by nurses and doctors standing over me. They stood over me, discussing the results, then, one by one, left the room. One nurse stayed and finished unhooking my needles. Begrudgingly I asked, "So now what?" She delicately replied, "Well, it depends on how well you manage the stress in your life." My sarcastic response was, "My stressful life is managing me. I have no control." Smiling, she responded, "I understand, but the stress in your life is taking a toll on your health." In my head, I thought, "Easy for you to say you're not in my life." She began sharing with me her stories; reluctantly, I shared a little of mine. We both listened to our sad chain of events, but neither one of us tried to solve each other's problems. Her only advice was to inform me that according to my chart if I continued to bleed due to stress, major surgery would be in my future. I have always been against surgery, but now, if that is the case, it seems I would have no choice. It was nice to be heard by someone who just listened, and obviously, the unloading appeared to be what we both needed.

Returning to a quiet empty home, my thoughts took me back to the lack of control and choices I had in my life. This was my third close call. Despite feeling depressed as if there was nothing I could do, the need for change was pounding through my head. It wasn't long before the family all came home, and dinner was made. Unlike the nights before, when dinner had been completely silent due to the last few days' events, dinner at our home was hardly ever dull. Most of the time it was very eventful.

"Dinner and a show" was how our meals together were best described. Everyone had something to share with whatever popped into their heads, and it was always random. As entertaining as it was, sometimes it could become very overwhelming. Sometimes the dinner conversation was mild and easy, and other times you felt like you had entered a Nascar race with everyone competing to be heard. Their bottled-up energy and excitement shined the most at dinner time. Knowing that everyone was comfortable with each other to let loose was a good thing, but could become somewhat stressful when not everyone was on the same page to receive it. Some nights my husband and I played referee or ring leaders in our own circus, while other nights we would join the circus just to

49

keep up. The hours I had in between my hospital visit that morning and evening dinner weren't enough rest for my mind and head for that night's dinner conversation, so this was going to be challenging for me. The children didn't mention the hospital visit which was fine I didn't want to worry them, and my husband briefly mentioned it. Due to his guilt surrounding what had been going on in our life, he was madder at himself than concerned with my details. Honestly, I didn't want to make him feel worse than he already did, so not discussing it worked out well for all of us. As we began to eat, one by one each person started to talk, not separately all together. Each story was different and the tones were small and grew louder as they talked. Everyone wanted and needed to be heard, especially over the top of each other. The chatter was so deafening that night it had affected me on a different level. Usually, I could play a good ping pong match with each person and actually hear them and pay attention even with all the background noise, but not tonight. No longer could I give anyone their full individual attention, it was all a blur of voices and faces. It was like being in a supersonic subway hearing the abundance of the different loud sounds, from people talking with fast-paced movements rushing around me frantically. The energy was so high that evening my brain couldn't keep up or register anything around me, and then my body slowly began to collapse. Immediately my husband noticed me shutting down and carefully walked me to the chair. By this point, everyone was quiet and alarmed, as I slowly closed my eyes and surrendered to the moment. Life and everything in it at that moment had consumed and overwhelmed me to my breaking point.

<u>Thoughts for Ashley:</u>

"When things get overwhelming please slow down, get quiet with yourself to allow your soul and heart to rest and reset enough to bounce back. Life is hard but our God is stronger, put everything in His hands."

Love Mom

CHAPTER TWELVE

Returning to Myself

"Finding yourself is not really how it works. You are not a ten dollar bill in last's winters coat pocket. You are also not lost. Your true self is right there, buried under cultural conditioning, other people's conclusions you drew as a kid that became your beliefs about who you are. Finding yourself is actually returning to yourself. An unlearning, an excavation, a remembering of who you were before the world got it's hands on you."

Emily Mcdowell

The nights that followed were filled with more dreams and nightmares, some new and ones that kept reoccurring. They became twisted and graphic to the point I was unable to get a good night's sleep for months; the only way I slept was with extra sleeping pills. Meanwhile, with the restraining order against his ex-wife in place for a year, our schedules had to change. Making adjustments to our day-to-day activities, we began to go about life differently. Without her in the picture, we all behaved diversely, cycles were being broken and everyone's patterns changed. Once the year was over and the judge instructed us to resume the old schedule, the anticipation had some of us on pins and needles, wondering how it would be. To my surprise, it was better; growth had evolved from everyone throughout that year. That is, everyone but me seemed to be able to move past what had happened. Returning to the counselor every other week as needed was suggested for all of us to continue healing; I was the only one still seeking help, that is, with a multitude of other issues as well. Upon one of our last sessions, his suggestion was to forgive myself and to focus on myself along with forgiving others for the past. Not fully understanding how this advice would help, the redirection onto myself seemed reasonable. Spending time alone doing something I enjoyed was never an option or a consideration; this would be a new adventure for me. In the following days, I made some appointments to do some major self-care. Even though this was new, it was kinda exciting. We own a seasonal restaurant, and during this time frame, we were closed for the season, so it was perfect timing to take some time for ourselves. Encouraging my husband to do the same, we both enjoyed focusing on ourselves for once. Knowing that we were on the same page, allowed us both to not feel guilty. With all of the trauma our whole family had encountered, he was under an incredible amount of stress himself. My husband is a passionate, beautiful man with a very loving soul, and his need for some time and space was badly needed, as was mine. Neither of us wanted to burden each other with our thoughts or feelings; we just knew how desperate we were in need of an escape from our reality. Despite the struggles and fights we had been going through, our love prevailed, and forgiveness replaced the guilt that we needed to find a new playground. With a supportive husband and my determination to take care of me, my new direction was underway. Spending days pampering myself by having massages, manicures, pedicures, and facials was nice but soon became costly. Regardless of the enjoyment I experienced, they were temporary moments. Boredom quickly set in, and I was craving something more meaningful and lasting for myself. So I began surfing the internet. With God's hands holding me, I found exactly what I needed a yoga instructor that changed my life forever. Our first phone call was very interesting, she was hesitant to answer my questions, and I was hesitant to ask them. Through many conversations, we realized we both had what each other had been searching for at this precise moment in life: a new direction to get back to our true authentic selves. She was indecisive about starting her private yoga sessions again due to her physical setbacks. As for me, I wasn't sure if this particular yoga/meditation place would satisfy my hunger for more since every other yoga class I had attended only provided the exercise portion. Once we began our sessions, I came to the conclusion this was way more than just yoga; it was the spiritual and emotional space where my healing was about to begin.

Walking in on my first day, expecting to see your typical yoga studio, I was pleasantly surprised. My eyes gazed back and forth, seeing shelves of incense, candles, and inspirational books that filled table after table. The alluring wall art and eye-catching macrame decorations had me beaming with delight while the smell of sage burning immersed my senses. Tranquilized by the calming atmosphere, I made my way down the hall to our room. My breath was taken away from all of the gorgeous tapestry hanging, colorful crystals and geodes on display, and a variety of natural elements in every corner.   Slowly sitting down on the incredibly soft shag carpet, my soul was ecstatic to embark on this new adventure. As soon as she joined me in the room, we both sat facing one another with our legs crisscrossed with pleasing smiles on our faces. After a few minutes of sharing the quiet moment, she asked me, "How are you feeling today?" I said, "I am nervous, feeling guarded, full of anxiety, and excited all at the same time." She asked the next question, "What is the one thing you would like to address today?" Without hesitation, my response was, "Teach me how to be in the same room or space with negative energy and intense anxiety from others and not absorb it." Seeing the demand in my request and my demeanor immediately change, she instructed me to close my eyes, then take a deep breath and slowly release it out through my nose. We repeated this several times until my body language shifted back to a calm composure. Once in a serene place, her concern was about where all of my negative energy was coming from. First, she asked, "Where in your body does it hurt?" Then the next question was, "Tell me what has been going on in your life that has been negative?" Feeling free to speak, the tears immediately ran down my cheeks as I unraveled my truth. Having this freeing moment was like unshackling chains that had been weighing me down for years. Expressing my words in greater depth than I had ever done with anyone, the more the confessions came out, the more I realized just how much I had been holding.

Blaming others for my discontentment, the unfairness in life that took my control, the tightness in my body from the undeserved stress people had thrust upon me, to the resentment of things not going my way, I noticed immediately my words sounded like complaining people in my life for which had made me disgusted. Her non-judgmental words spilled out fiercely with compassion for my pain and enlightenment for my soul. She gave me a few illustrations, never suggesting my ignorance of life, just simply stating the obvious, which piqued my curiosity to learn more. Her style lured me to engage with more conversion; the need to understand had my full attention. Conditional happiness was introduced, along with the statements, "You can't control what other people say or do, and they can't control you" and "You can't be responsible for how other people react to what you say or do." Being a "good girl" to please others and keep the peace will only shut down your throat chakra, ultimately making you appear small with no voice. In regard to blocking their negative energy, being a sensitive empath and giving too much allowed my openness to letting everything in. I needed to learn how to be in the moment and block out all bad energy by having boundaries. To which I replied, "Teach me how." Suddenly dialogue stopped, and we began slow Vinyasa positions dedicated to flow and breathe work. Next, we did poses known as Ansas, which were followed by a meditation period. As she guided me through the meditation, asking specific questions and pushing for me a release, all of my pinned-up emotions poured out, along with a tremendous amount of crying. Coming to the close of our session, we did a pose called Savasana which was my final resting period. Becoming relaxed, I fell into a deep sleep, for which she allowed me to wake up on my own. Awaking sometime later and feeling slightly embarrassed about falling asleep, my body felt so light from the heavy load that had been taken off. The contentment refreshed my soul in such a way that happiness flooded my heart where it had been lost. Slowly making my way to the hallway where we met, there were some other women gathered around. One woman said to me, "I think you found your safe place." While another replied, "Remember, yoga isn't just about tightening your a**, it's about getting your head out of it." Walking out with a smile on my face, I was eager for our next session.

Counting the hours until our next session, I practiced every pose she had taught me and thought about the stories that had been discussed. Coming into our next session was the introduction of several books suggested for me to read, conveniently she had them all in her shop. We read a few paragraphs from a few a them. The one that sat with me that day was from <u>Warrior Goddess Training</u> by Heather Ash Amara. Here's what she read, "The truth is simple: Life is perfectly imperfect, unpredictable, and unexplainable. A Warrior Goddess does not try to control life or even understand it. Our job is to consciously choose what we are aligning with and then let go and dance in joy and gratitude for every moment of existence." As straightforward as that was to hear, it seemed tough to do. Connecting with those words, she asked, "Tell me where your body hurts today?" Not sure the direction she was heading, I replied, "My neck, hips, legs, and I have been heavily bleeding for months and with terrible cramps." Explaining my many visits to the hospital over excessive bleeding, she nodded and picked up a different book. As she read from a different book, she stated short emotional facts that can cause the body to hurt in these areas. Here were some of those facts: fear, stopping the process of life, inflexibility and guilt, lack of ability to receive pleasure, blood representing joy in the body flowing freely, lack of joy, stubbornly holding on to the pain of the past, self, rejecting femininity, fear of future, and not wanting to move forward. After hearing these, I became very quiet. Astonished by the accuracy, I asked, "What book is that one?" She said, "<u>You can heal your life</u> by Louise Hay." Giving thought to the last visit to the hospital, I remembered my conversation with the nurse. My emotional and physical well-being cannot and should not be dependent on what others say or do. Protective boundaries must be set; my body was reflecting my mental pain. Diving into a few poses and finishing with a meditation, we wrapped up our session. Leaving that day, she handed the books we had read a little from along with one more. A book written by Don Miguel Ruiz, <u>The Four Agreements</u>. Starring at that book, I smiled smugly; a customer of ours had been trying to get me to read this for over a year now. Taking a deep breath and sighing, I guess there was no choice this time. From a person who hated to read and hardly ever finished reading books, now books and research were what I longed for every day. The difference was it was for me this time, and my curiosity to understand more about helping myself became my goal.

<u>Thoughts for Ashley:</u>

Kurt Vonnegut, JR. wrote "Be soft. Do not let the world make you hard. Do not let pain make you hate. Do not let the bitterness steal your sweetness." Try to live by this quote.

Love Mom

CHAPTER THIRTEEN

Freedom From my Unwanted Guests

"Negative emotions are like unwelcome guests. Just because they show up on your doorstep doesn't mean they have a right to stay."

Deepak Chopra

Before my many yoga/meditation experiences, I would leave my home in an effort to be alone and gather my thoughts. While driving around looking for the perfect place to park or walk, my anxiety would build up, desperate to find answers, now thanks to my beautiful discovery, I can stay home in my "Zen Den" when needing an escape or read a book to help me sort through my emotions and feelings. Finding a new outlet has been life-changing. To return to yourself, you must slow down enough to see and hear yourself clearly. Before, I would stay so busy trying to ignore my issues and push everything under a rug that the only result I would have was exhaustion and frustration. Being busy was more of a distraction than a healer for me. Doing more didn't solve anything nor get me more attention. Instead, my overdoing left me with unsatisfied needs for myself and expectations from others when I stopped. There was nothing to prove by the over-investing I did in others; this not only enabled them but myself. It is one thing to be invested in the ones you love, but to rush at any given moment due to obligation is quite destructive. When I was not busy, I felt worthless and lazy, as if I had to keep up with the world's rat race was a requirement I had to fulfill. Others might look at me differently, get angry at me, or worse, abandon me; all these negative emotions surfaced out of fear and anxiety as I played back my past experiences. The fear of rejection would lead to fear of not being enough; in that battle, I thought I wasn't good enough or that I would disappoint everyone. How stupid I began to feel as I started thinking about all the times I overextended myself, misplacing it for simply being "the good girl," not noticing my desire was to be loved and accepted. That all needed to stop, time to change those choices. Drawn to the books I had obtained, I decided to spend the afternoon reading about more of these negative feelings I had been harboring. Oh, what many lessons I was learning through reading, yoga practices, meditations, and my own self-discovery. As my sessions increased my yoga teacher would add a few more resources to help with my journey, such as joining her book club. To openly discuss the same book with people and hear their feedback was exciting to me. Once she told us which book we were going to start with, I couldn't wait to start to get home to read it. Finishing the book <u>The Four Agreements</u> the night before, I was speechless about what I had unraveled about myself and couldn't wait to share my thoughts. Over the next few weeks, all of us in the club had compassion for each other as we listened to one another's stories and perspectives. Having several different points of view helped me understand the reasons behind some of my actions and see them from different angles. Attending more book clubs over the next few months and developing a better way of life for myself was allowing me to get stronger as I was healing. Our sessions grew more intense with movements and meditations, the unnecessary baggage I had been carrying was slowly unpacking. Between the words and the dreams that penetrated my mind, seeking answers to benefit my existence and learning how to block all negativity was my new discovery. After much exploration and the release of bound emotions, slowly, I began to figure out how important it was to love myself. Playing a victim role and the blame game had been my life's story. Having a whole new perspective through gratitude and awareness made forgiveness and letting go an easier concept to try. Living up to expectation after expectation, I assumed others would do the same. When they did not meet my expectations, I would take it personally and get hurt.

Getting acknowledgment or approval were things I assumed would return to me through love and attention from others. Taking people at their word and never noticing the actions behind their words turned out to be huge disappointments. You should never listen to what people say, only the actions behind their words. What you allow to resonate is what you will mirror outward. When my life got flipped upside down, my mind was exposed to negativity, and not being strong enough to fight it off, I would allow all of it to dwell inside. I was going against myself by blaming and judging myself for not living up to other's beliefs. Here's an example of believing another's opinion: I was told when I chewed and ate like a cow, which embarrassed me enough to cover my mouth in public every time I ate a meal. Years later, a loved one asked why I covered up my mouth when I ate, so I explained. He removed my hand from my face and told me it wasn't true, then asked me never to cover it again so everyone would see my beautiful face. Those hurtful words became my thoughts which turned into my beliefs and resulted in my actions. I had changed my behavior due to the opinions of others about me without any hesitation or thought of my own. A hard lesson I had to learn was that you should never take anything personally. That being the case, every good or bad situation that had happened in my life was about them, not me. People are in a completely different world in their own minds; reacting to their thoughts, beliefs, and feelings is never about you. Everything that is said or done to you has nothing to do with you. Taking things personally from others will allow their seeds of doubt and fear to enter your healthy mind, which in turn fills your mind with their emotional weeds in your garden life. Getting upset about something or someone for hurting you is only a reflection of your own fears, insecurities, and worries. Of course, getting your feelings hurt is natural, but your reaction is what will determine how it will play out in your life. You should acknowledge it, feel the emotion, react calmly, address it if necessary, and then let it go. Remember it is not anyone's job but yours to take care of yourself and provide your own happiness. Powerless from wrestling with my inner judge and victim, only to try to see my unworthiness had me exhausted. My relationships had suffered because of my need to seek attention and approval from outside resources instead of searching within. Constantly living in a world that was good one minute and could blow up the next, I was mentally and physically frozen most of the time. Allowing the moods of others around me to have an influence, I began trying to figure out my next step from their direction. This was my roller coaster from hell that I rode daily.

Without having a sense of love for myself, I would assume from their words what their actions would be. Like I have always said to my kids. "Never assume because it will make an a** out of you and me." Yet another piece of advice I never took for myself. Since my alarms were easily triggered by the anticipation of when the next storm was going to happen, the people in my life were not receiving my true self and never knew the anxiety I experienced on a daily basis. The true authentic me was locked away for safety and silenced for fear of setting any bombs off unnecessarily. I couldn't relax anymore because safety was more important than connection. I was in survival mode, disassociated from the world. Letting my guard down meant not being prepared for whatever came crashing down. I stopped trusting life and felt like I was on watch duty every day, waiting for the next attack. I couldn't love myself fully which made it impossible to share love with others, hence my relationships started to suffer. Until I decided to love myself again, but correctly this time, take care of myself to ensure good self-care, figure out what I wanted and needed in life, and then go after it; then things began to come together. This was a slow process since years had gone by with the people in my life taking for granted the needs I had never discussed, solely due to my inability to express myself or communicate my needs. Everyone assumed I was good. I ran across this quote about self-worth that summed it up perfectly. This is written by Doe Zantamata "When you try to make things better for a lot of people, you may end up making things worse for yourself. A little self-sacrifice is noble, but depriving yourself of too much will only leave you depleted. By that time, most people won't even realize that you need anything because you're the one who has always given. Take care of yourself. Self-preservation is not selfish; it's essential for living a full and happy life."

All these years of repressed emotions that tortured my mind and body were nothing but thoughts and opinions of others I had allowed to turn into my beliefs. I was living in my own mental hell created by demons who I gave permission to speak and dwell inside my body. All of the false statements and beliefs had left me blind to the truth. I was searching outwards instead of inwards, where I already had everything I needed. I had created an image to be perfect and to meet the satisfaction of others while rejecting myself. The first person I needed to forgive was myself. I had molded myself to suit others' wants or needs only to hide from my true authentic self, being tolerant by saying "yes" when I should have said "no." Self-abandonment seemed to be the hot button for my lack of self-worth; focusing more on the needs of others was ingrained in me like a carving on an old oak tree that you could see 20 years later.

With one of the many deep meditation sessions we had been through, I remember the one that helped me cope with the incident that occurred at my home with his ex-wife. Explaining in detail what had happened to us that morning, my yoga instructor knew exactly what questions to ask as I drifted into my meditation that day. As the answers to her questions were given, my body temperature rose, and I began to shake and tremble. She took me into her eyes to feel what she was feeling that morning, not through my eyes, which was unexpected. They weren't hard questions, it was the answers that came that were hard to hear. Here is where my mind went as I recall - Traveling back to what she might have been feeling that day, I knew she was in her manic state that morning. Because I had experienced this before in other people and had been told of past events in which she had displayed similar acts, I felt like I knew what behavior was to be expected and why. I knew her mood was elevated, her level of energy was high, her focus was on me as the enemy, and her goal was to retrieve her son. In this type of situation, there is no reasoning; you hope for the best and that they will quickly get through without harming themselves or others. Since this incident was not as violent as her other times before, the anticipation of a twist at any moment had me concerned. I had never participated with a person during this kind of manic state; the stakes were higher for me since I was the one who had the target on their back. Going back and reliving this moment put my body in a state of panic and fear, just as I was that morning, which caused my anger to come alive inside me. As quickly as I felt robbed of my safety and security, something inside of me suddenly shifted to compassion for her. Imagining how she must have felt being so out of control, she probably didn't even realize where she was or how she got there. I might not have had control in that moment, but I could get control where she couldn't; she must have been just as scared. When a person hurts someone verbally or physically, they are hurting themselves. I can't imagine the pain she must have felt that day, as her actions spoke for her feelings.

How could I stay mad or hold a grudge? It will only steal my happiness and keep me from moving forward. She was acting out her emotions through her fear and her anger, and by the only way, she knew how to be in that moment. Even though her actions were directed towards others, it was her internal battle she was trying to fight. God placed His hands on me at that moment and guided me away from anger and into love through my meditation. Shivering from sweat but calm and in a serene place in my mind, we were done, so I gathered my belongings to leave. Not a word was spoken as we exchanged small quaint smiles, both knowing something beautiful had just taken place.

Upon arriving home, I rushed in to take advantage of my time alone to reflect on the revealing meditation I had just experienced. Taken back by the nightmares over the last few nights, seeing the intruders in my mind, my unwanted guests, and feeling what she might have felt that morning, I was drawn to one of my daily readings from the Bible. Immediately I looked up Matthew 6:14-15. It says, "For if you forgive other people when they sin against you, your heavenly Father will also forgive you. But if you do not forgive others their sins, your Father will not forgive your sins." Next, I grabbed my book of quotes, looking for another inspiring quote from Doe Zantamata. Here is what she had to say "Anyone can hold a grudge, but it takes a person of character to forgive. When you forgive, you release yourself from the painful burden. Forgiveness doesn't mean what happened was OK, and it doesn't mean that person should still be welcome in your life. It just means you have made peace with the pain and are ready to let go."

<u>Thoughts for Ashley:</u>

"Please never allow the past to take residence in your mind for too long. Holding on to the past will only hurt you and prevent you from growing into the beautiful woman you are. God has given you special gifts to share with the world. Forgive, heal, and keep moving through this wonderful life God gave us. Remember – sometimes we don't get to throw people away or out of our lives like garbage, but we can pray and hope that they will recycle well if we have no choice but to have them in our lives."

Love Mom

CHAPTER FOURTEEN

Taking Back my Sunshine

"Clearing and releasing negative emotions, core issues, fear, anxiety, etc. simply removes the blocks to your natural tendency to shine. You matter. You have a gift to give to the world."

Ginny Walker

Countless days and nights went by with session after session, I was regaining my confidence and was beginning to shine brighter from the inside out. Life was better than it had been in years. The last time I felt this good was the year of my Cinderella story with my husband, except this time, I was doing it all on my own. Through his words and actions, he made me feel beautiful just the way I was. His love and affection kept proving to me that I was more than enough to be loved. Now it was my turn to do that for myself. No more self-abandonment, no more blaming or guilt, no more anger in my heart, only love in the present, knowing I was enough. Through several more deep, intense meditations, I began unraveling each and every pain from my past, peeling layer after layer off of the heavy loads that had been holding me down. Each time I felt freer and lighter, the weight of darkness was coming off. From a person who always needed to know the answers and details to believing that not knowing everything was the key to releasing anger seemed unheard of to me. Being at peace with the unknown felt quite impossible for me to achieve. This was until I made meditation a daily practice and strived to become a master of letting go. Once I learned how to use meditation as a way to completely be in the moment with one's self and release all thoughts, I could then start to let go of all of the stress that engulfed my life. Spending an entire weekend building my own "Zen Den" helped me design a special place all about me. I had never had my own space or been able to decorate with only me in mind. It was time to take everything I had learned and practice at home. My "Zen Den" turned out to be a warm, cozy, and peaceful place. The perfect space to retreat from the world's troubles. Sitting in my special place, I tried to reflect back to all of the good moments when I was truly happy with myself and life in general and realized the bad moments completely outweighed the good ones. Over time I quit the fight to make good moments happen and had allowed the terrible times to take over. Sometimes, it was easier that way; the deep dark hole they had fallen into was now where I had landed. Becoming a slave to others and their moods had changed me; I was suffering right along with them. Wishing I could climb out was impossible since I was full of self-rejection and a lack of self-acceptance while others were draining my cup, and I was doing nothing for myself to keep it full. No one was coming to save me, and waiting for someone to give me support was pointless.

Giving thought to my most recent dream, the connection and purpose were coming together. In my dream, I was on the beach, sitting at the end of a pier, looking out into the ocean; ahead of me, I saw the sun barely rising above the horizon. To the right of me, there were storm clouds off in the distance slowly moving in as the waves were crashing about tossing bottles up and down within each current. To the left of me was darkness; the water was calm, with rippled waves carrying broken pieces of debris scattered all across the ocean. As I gaze around me, a sense of numbness embraces my soul. All is quiet in my head; not a single thought is present, and no emotions are evolving. After a few minutes, the silence was broken by the sound of nature's voices as they surrounded me. Feeling the urge to stand up and soak it all in, my attention quickly shifts to a familiar voice behind me. As I turned around, there she was, Ashley, staring lovely at me. Hearing her call out to me, "It's me, mom," we smile at each other. As we walk towards each other, the pier begins to collapse and break apart. Nature was getting louder, and the storms were closing in. We both came to a dead stop in our tracks, and expressions of discouragement filled our faces. She screams over the banging and cracking of the pier, "Please forgive yourself. It was not your fault, nor was it their fault; life happens, and we all have to forgive and move on. Don't repeat your past; face it, break the cycles and patterns, and finally, let go. Face your mirrors and set yourself free; let the world see your sunshine again." With the pier falling out from under us both, her last words were, "I love you, Mom, and I'll always be with you." As she faded away with the broken pieces of wood, I was left dangling from the edge of the last leg standing from the pier. It didn't take long for the last part of the pier to wash away; then, the current rushed me into the ocean. Somehow thrashing through the waves, I managed to wash up onto the beach. Gathering myself, I noticed the shoreline where I had landed was covered by the bottles and debris from the ocean that had washed up along with me. Overwhelmed by all that had taken place, I took a deep long breath and, on my exhale, looked straight ahead to realize the sun was at a standstill. Through all the storms and madness of the ocean, it was in the same spot. Thinking about Ashley's words, I began to lie down with the bottles nudging up against me. Curious, I began opening the bottles; each one had a message inside them. Going through each bottle, I found a different memory, trauma, disappointment, and loss from my past. Upon reading each one, I journeyed back in time to revisit, relive, and acknowledge each event and began seeing them in different ways, which led to understanding the lessons better, but the bitterness was still resenting inside me, wanting an apology or revenge for what they had done. Having to dig deep to forgive was difficult, but it hit me that just because they hadn't expressed their feelings didn't mean God hadn't dealt with them. After all, putting it in His hands allows us to let go and for Him to handle it for us. If we can't let go, He can't do His job. Once again, Ashley's words were running through my head as I took each bottle and looked back and experienced each traumatic and hurtful event all over again, only to feel it, release it, and begin the healing process through forgiveness once and for all. I knew she was right, but reflecting and letting go was hard. Desperate to find my inner joy and happiness and to put back the missing pieces I had lost, I decided to reframe the old stories. By reframing or retelling my old stories, I could hopefully see the good in the experiences God had given me and allow myself to learn the lessons God was trying to teach me along the way. Due to focusing only on the negative feelings each experience had left me before reframing them, I knew I had been blinded to see them for what they truly were, but now I could see and grow from my new stories. Once you look through the eyes of others, your heart creates a place in it for gratitude and appreciation for what had happened to you and them; never seeing a different side of the story, you stay stuck. It is like when a psychiatrist holds up a picture and asks, "What do you see?" every person sees something different from their own perspective. Sometimes we need to look at things from every angle, not just one. Learning how to be present in the moment creates an awareness not only of the people you are with but also of the details of your surroundings. Once you become aware then life can appear differently through your eyes, and clarity will start to show up. Through my awareness and reframing of past stories, new and positive life lessons took the place of the painful ones. I began realizing how my bad experiences didn't mold me into a worthless human being, but instead, they built my character and gave me the resilience to handle whatever life threw at me, and the good experiences gave me memories. Continuing to go through each bottle, my spirit was overjoyed by the release of negativity that was replaced with compassion and forgiveness. One by one, I fiercely tore apart each event and was determined to find only the good in each one, swearing off the painful ones to never take residence in my head again. As the clouds took up less space in the sky, so did the darkness in my soul. Proudly, I declared happiness and love for myself and gave myself permission to have a voice to be heard, not silenced. Cleaning up the cobwebs in my mind and clutter from the world I once lived in was liberating and freeing. Slowly the garbage inside of me and around me was disappearing. I will no longer raise a white flag to defeat over my battles; I am worth fighting for. You will see me coming not going away from situations, no longer watching my shadows fade into the darkness when trouble arises. Once the last bottle was addressed, a sigh of relief consumed my body. I closed my eyes and thanked God for the heaviness that had been lifted that day. Opening my eyes, I was met with the brightness of the sun fully shining with its magnificent array of colors; my sunshine was coming back in front of me and inside of me. Surrounding me was an abundance of butterflies fluttering in swarms filling the blue sky above me. Butterflies give the perfect example of rebirth and that new beginnings do exist, for they go through darkness to get to light just as we need to. God's love and mercy demonstrate how our transformation is possible and better when we allow Him to work in our lives. If, when we are in our metamorphism stage, we can trust and believe in His perfect timing, only then will life get better. Putting faith and trust in God can be hard at times, as we all know, but we are not equipped to handle it on our own. Through patience and the changing of cycles, along with developing harmony and balance, we can become like nature, following the path for which God created us. Seeing the butterflies gave me such peace that, at that moment, I realized Ashley and I had switched places that day. Her fading away was replaced with images of myself or, as I figured out later, my "inner" child, which had been speaking to me through her and needed to be heard, seen, and loved.

Even though that was the last time she appeared in my dreams, I do know she will always be with me in my heart. Having that kind of peace in my heart was amazing, keeping my peace would be the challenge. Picking up painful stories or having negative thoughts can rob you of your daily peace if you allow it. The mind is like the ocean on the surface. It can be still and calm, but underneath, there is nothing but busy activity going on. Being present at the moment can prevent some of this busy activity from taking residence in your mind, but we have to become mindful of what should stay or go. Being the gatekeeper of your mind only has to be as hard as you make it. Human beings are naturally wired to obtain information and get lost in thinking, especially in this digital rat race of the world we live in, but keeping up or staying busy doesn't produce happiness or peace. It only creates suffering for yourself because your "We Are Open 24 Hours" sign never shuts off. Your mind doesn't stand a chance of ever fully relaxing or having peace until you take down the sign and make your "Monkey Mind" behave. Being mindful of taking the peace you deserve when you need it will require some major self-control and maybe even some adjustments in your lifestyle. As for me, I needed some intense house cleaning along with breaking some patterns and stopping bad cycles that I continued to allow in my life that were stealing my peace.

<u>Quotes for Myself:</u>

"I know you carry deep wounds, and sometimes you act out your unhealed pain. Offer yourself compassion but then commit to doing better. Once we know better, there's no excuse not to do better. What we don't heal will be passed on through our generations."

Ash Alves

"She was a forgiver. Her heart was so large she didn't know how to give up on people, because she always believed the good in those she loved. It wasn't until she was walked on so many times she had no choice but to let go of those who burned holes in her heart."

C.R. Bittar

CHAPTER FIFTEEN

Confession is Good For The Soul

"Be the person who breaks the cycle. If you were judged, choose understanding. If you were rejected, choose acceptance. If you were shamed, choose compassion. Be the person you needed when you were hurting, not the person who hurt you. Vow to be better than what broke you, to heal inside instead of becoming bitter so you can act from your heart, not your pain."

Lori Deschene

For Christmas one year, my husband bought me a new pair of binoculars; these had a special feature that could be fine-tuned for people wearing glasses. I was so excited to use them, I could hardly wait for our next hunting trip; the first thing I did was pull them out and make the necessary adjustments. Once my eyes looked through them, I was shocked at how clear everything had become, and I was amazed by all of the details that surrounded me. The woods never seemed so beautiful as they did that day; I spent the rest of the afternoon looking through my binoculars and taking it all in. I spent years using my old pair, never once questioning its clarity or thinking it was time for a new pair. It's ironic how we can go through life in a fog accepting the bare minimum and never truly seeing what more life might have to offer us, and only when we are given a new set of lenses or perspective can we truly see. Our hunting had come to an end for the weekend; we began our 8-

hour trip back home. Finishing the book I had started before the trip about John Lennon's life, the Beatles song "Strawberry Fields Forever" came to my mind at that moment. Here are the words that stuck out to me "Living is easy with eyes closed. Misunderstanding is all you see. It's getting hard to be someone, but it all works out. It doesn't matter much to me." Think about that for a minute: how easy is it to just accept life as it is, never question what it could be, and find yourself settling? From a person needing to understand, finding out more of the answers to my unresolved issues was imperative for me to know. Having hours in front of me, I decided to reflect on a few situations that had recently happened from this trip and had me left full of anxiety and not sure why. Little did I know what my awareness was about to show me wouldn't be pretty. The bad thing about becoming aware of something is once you are aware you can never be unaware.

Over the last few days, I have been around several familiar people, and I noticed a shift in my personality as I became a different person. I felt like I did over a year again when I started my yoga class trying to cope with a room full of negativity that wasn't mine. With all of the revisiting, releasing, and forgiveness I had been through, I thought I was in a good place to deal with whatever was thrown at me. With my invisible bubble around me to protect myself thinking I was safe, the thought never crossed my mind that it was me that I needed protection from. I had become an automatic pilot, handling every situation the same as I had done before, never veering from the old paths I once traveled. Distress and panic grew inside me, tugging at me to change old patterns and needing to know how. Once I pondered each isolated situation, I realized it wasn't just about me changing to suit each individual mood as they changed; it was about me not staying true to myself and how I felt. I needed to stop becoming a chameleon who adjusted to each environment as the people around me changed. I was now wearing their dirty glasses. Unconsciously, I went into fix-it mode to adjust their mood back to being happy so things were always good for everyone involved. I was an emotional sponge soaking up every drop of emotional poison they would gush out, with no regard to how I felt or should feel, as I took on their emotions, disregarding my feelings. Once again, as they would feel better, I became drained from taking on their nasty energy. It wasn't enough to just block them or ignore them, I needed to be stronger and more confident in being myself no matter what type of room I walked into. The other issue I encountered was not being able to share my exciting news about my new ventures with yoga that had brought me happiness with everyone that weekend; I kept it all inside for fear of depressing them since they were in a bad place to receive anything good. Allow me to give you an example of how I went from being happy to sharing anything and everything to clamming up most of the time and holding it all in, which led to losing many mini happy dances of my life. Imagine for the last few years you had been all bubbly and lively every day at your work, and everyone looked forward to embracing it. One day, all changed. You walked in and cracked a funny joke, but no one laughed, and instead, you gave a scowl for being funny. Everyone is sober like they just left a funeral. Questioning the atmosphere, no one seemed to have an answer, and you left wondering whether you should continue your happy demeanor. The next day, you try again to be happy with everyone, but this time, they look at you like you are crazy. You approach a table where the same customers had come there for years and always had a conversation with you and loved your joyful spirit, and they avoid you and treat you like a stranger who just barged into their home trying to sell them something. Most of the time, when others talk, you don't mind and encourage it, but it is nice when people take an interest in you and what you have to say as well. Conversation is only allowed when the focus is on or about them or when their mood is good. You're allowed to interact or hang around and join the group; it is about their comfort level, not yours. Do these things over and over again with people and get nothing back; you will eventually stop trying to be happy in their presence or communicate anything positive because if it is not acknowledged, you will be left feeling uncomfortable and confused about how to act or be. Your communication will go to nothing, and your presence will disappear. Again all to help them feel comfortable at the expense of your own discomfort. Trying to be the nice person by not rubbing in all the good things life had given me, resulted in not sharing or celebrating with people around me. This conditioned my brain to not be happy all the time; only if something really great happened then could I just maybe celebrate, but only if those around me could embrace it with love and excitement. This was definitely not who I truly was; I'm the positive half-glass-full type of person. I could see good in every bad situation and was the one who could encourage others to see the same, but now I was wearing their dirty glasses and afraid to share anything. This revelation inferior-ted me when I became aware of my actions; this led me to uncover the real reason I wasn't feeling happy anymore. I was the one who brought sunshine to the room; now, I was the one looking for it. I was the one always smiling and laughing, enjoying everything in life, whether good or bad. That pattern of checking the temperature before you get into the pool approach should not have been the approach I used when sharing happy or good news when wanting to share it, but unfortunately, I had adapted it. The people in my life should celebrate with me, not disregard it like it was nothing. Now, this wasn't the case with all of my friends or family, just a few. Realizing I hadn't fully addressed these blocks, an urgency to break cycles and change patterns suddenly became my new priority. I was avoiding conflict to keep peace, by starting a war inside myself. Here's an example of what came to mind of how I used to be: put yourself looking over a stadium from the sky watching a Garth Brooke concert. Now zoom in and look at the crowd, everyone is standing still and quiet. This is very unusual considering who is performing, they should be dancing, singing, and screaming. Zoom in closer to a specific group, now here's where I see my old self. She would have been slowly shaking her hips while looking around for others to join. Then after five minutes in she would have just gone for it and danced with no care in the world for what others thought or did. Oh, how I miss that woman. Creating a new pattern would require balancing other people's needs and your own to create harmony for yourself and others. The problem was I had put so much focus on everyone else in my life that knowing what I wasn't visible. Putting all your focus on someone else robs you from focusing on yourself, and is a complete waste of time and energy. Imagine walking into a new restaurant that you have never been before. You sit down and never actually order just point at the menu over multiple choices. You have the expectation that the server would know what you wanted to eat, and after waiting 30 minutes to find out that the order never got sent in because you weren't clear on which item. You get impatient and mad because you were waiting on someone else to read your mind, and the server assumed you hadn't made a decision. Without clear communication, you are upset. By not clearly telling them what you wanted to eat, you decide to leave and they are confused. Who is wrong here? Having an unrealistic expectation with someone or something happening is ridiculous, and will lead to dissatisfaction and disappointment.

Having too many unrealistic expectations all of the time can be unbearable, and will lead to the destruction of any relationship if unresolved. All this time I looked at expectations as only something one shouldn't count on in life to fulfill for us, and never saw that I was putting expectations on others in a way to return all the good I had given to them. Sitting with that thought made me ponder over different situations and understand clearly why I stayed upset and was so angry. No one was going to fulfill my expectations, no different than the restaurant story they can't read someone's mind and you have a voice for reason. I do have a voice to be heard, no matter if it is good news or bad news; it wasn't for me to worry about how they interrupted what I said. My job was to speak the truth and be honest about how I felt when I felt it and not hold back to spare their feelings, you can't blame them for you not owning your role in the situation, it's your job, not theirs. The inconsistency that was all around me was driving me crazy, to the point that all of my good behaviors were nonexistent, and I was mirroring out their behaviors or, even worse, creating bad ones of my own. Wanting to scream in the car but couldn't, my mind kept going forward to more issues for me to address within myself. Getting to the root cause would help keep the awful thoughts from spinning around in my head and I could avoid making the same mistakes over and over again. Lack of love and self-worth for myself kept showing up, I knew it had been part of the reason I kept repeating these cycles. So grabbing a hold of my mind and deciding to tackle each one, I re-group with what I had learned. My monkey brain and I were in a state of emergency, and I needed to get my head out of my a** to fix it. The first step is to bring my awareness to every situation and dissect it for what it was. Next, decide whose emotion is it and only take it on if you feel the same, and then learn how to manage your emotions. This goes back to mindfulness, you observe the situation, feel it, and don't allow it to penetrate you so much to change your behavior. The biggest lesson I hadn't learned yet was setting proper boundaries, I wish I had done this before the trip it could have kept me from sinking so low.

<u>Thoughts for Myself:</u>

"Very little is needed to make a happy life; it is all within yourself, in your way of thinking."

Marcus Aurelius Antoninus

"When something I can't control happens, I ask myself; where is the hidden gift, where is the positive in this?"

Sara Blakely

CHAPTER SIXTEEN

Building My Bridges Back

"I demolish my bridges behind me – then there is no choice but to move forward."

Lori Deschene

"Hopefully, we can build bridges, but we also have to draw lines."

Fred Thompson

During my next yoga/meditation session, I mentioned all that had happened over my weekend. This led to many questions on how to get over this stage I thought I had passed. After listening to my stories, she reminded me that we will always be students learning every day. These return situations are repeating themselves because they are mirroring back to you your thoughts and how you see yourself. Past hurts, and beliefs are learned behaviors that can be unlearned. We shouldn't attack the person we need to address the problem. This session turned into a well-needed counseling session for me to get back on track. Here's what I learned. Every day, it's important to bring our awareness to what we are thinking about at the moment and where we are placing our energy to spot a trigger before it takes residence in our minds. When you walk around with a mind full of complaints, stress, or resentment, you will drain your positive, loving thoughts; without those good thoughts, you will feel heavy and less connected. To handle life in general or any relationship, you need to have a positive mental attitude so you can have more energy and clarity to handle any situations that will arise. The bright glare from all of the mirrors reflecting at me was shining a light so bright I couldn't help but see my inner child screaming at me as I could hear her say, "Do you see yourself in them?" All of my wounded emotions and past experiences I kept carrying around with me were seeping into my present-day life, causing more frustration than needed. She gave me three questions to ask myself the next time I was faced with thinking before speaking: 1- Are my words going to be kind to what I am about to say? 2- Will they be kind to me? 3-Is this history repeating itself, and am I about to repeat a bad pattern? Hmmm... some good questions, that would be my next exercise to practice. We shifted to meditation by bringing awareness to my focus, and then we discussed where I had been storing all my energy; that was an eye-opening process and hard to realize. Once you understand what you focus on, you will get more of my perspective on the way I had been thinking needed an overhaul quickly. Just forgiving the past wasn't enough; I needed to find the good in it so I could replace resentment with gratitude and focus on the positive. When I was able to shift from gratitude to love for the situation, everything changed; now, I could see good qualities instead of only the bad ones. Through my awareness, I discovered that many of my problems or issues I couldn't seem to get past were a result of my brooding and negativity. All of the issues stemmed back to my lack of control over the situation, or they had changed without my being ready for them, too. So silly that I look back and think how I had blamed them and taken on the victim role so easily, only to never see the good that had actually resulted from the terrible events. Now seeing not only through their eyes but through grateful eyes, I could see the good from every bad event I had dealt with and was blessed for it.

Next, we ventured into how to take on my responsibilities and let others take care of their own while making the necessary changes that would improve my mind, body, and soul. Her question for me was, "Define what it means for you to be a good person, partner, parent, or any other role that you have, then decide how you will go about it in the best way possible to suit your needs and desires, not others." What a loaded question, I thought. She didn't expect me to have an answer right then; it was understood she had given me homework to discuss for our next session. She followed with additional words to remember and take with me as I indulged in this assignment deeper; here is what she said: "Remember to stay in your own lane and never swerve into someone's lane, let them drive in their own lane and make their own mistakes. Don't let others get in the way of making these adjustments to find your balance in any area of your life. Others will not like your positive change, but over time, they will love you for being you if they are to have a place in your life. When you put yourself first, people might be disappointed and make you feel guilty due to the change, but let them. They need space to process their hurt and emotions and allow them to choose how they need to deal with it, and above all don't take it personally. Feeling guilty doesn't mean you're wrong; it means you're breaking free, can love them more, and still care. It's true that a person can be disappointed by you putting yourself first but still love you. Change is good; it means you are growing. It means you're moving forward, especially when it's for your own good. Never believe what others say or do has something to do with you; it never does. Don't take responsibility for fixing them or their situation; it's their job, not yours. Expect nothing from others and be grateful for everything life has given you. Having zero expectations will allow you to have a life of happiness. Take life just as it comes and flow with it like waves in the ocean. Never try to change anyone; only change how you deal with them. Realize you are enough, love yourself, and that the world cannot give you what you need, that is your job. You have everything you need inside you."

With some much information given to me that morning, the need for a nap before the kids got home was going to be required. Arriving home, I went straight upstairs, climbed into bed, and passed out from mental exhaustion. Resting for only a little bit, my eyes began to hurt and burn. As I tried to open them, they didn't budge. Alarmed, I got up, feeling my way around my bed, trying to make it to the bathroom. Desperate to open them and stop the pain, tears began flooding my face. No amount of trying was helping them to open; completely scared and upset, I fell to the floor and sat crying. Thinking back to what might have happened, the only other thing I had done that day was stop at the grocery store before getting home. Then I remembered how bright the sun had been as I stood in the checkout line and the conversation I had with the cashier telling her how I couldn't see the card reader because of the brightness of the sun. The grocery store didn't have a solid wood or metal roof. It was made of all glass windows. So, as I looked up and stared directly into the bright sun for at least a few minutes, who would have thought I might have done damage from doing that? As a sun lover, I relished at any moment I could be in the sun, so I loved looking up at it, especially that day because it was late winter and this was the first day the sun had been out in months. I sat for hours in pain, never able to open my eyes, and after finally making my way back to bed, I eventually fell asleep. I didn't sleep for long due to some dreams invading my sleep. The dream I had was mixed with parts of my past and a reoccurring dream that had shown up shortly after starting my yoga sessions. Let me take you into my dreams that night. The ocean was fierce, with rolling waves crashing against a ragged old ship where I was the captain, trying to navigate my way through the rough sea to an island I could barely see. On board, I had a variety of animals; they were so tightly crammed in that because of their discomfort they stayed upset and agitated, so most of the time, they were fighting each other. It was pitch dark, and with no stars in sight, the only light to see was a distant beam of strobing light from a lighthouse on the island. Between the animals fighting, the ship thrashing against the ocean, and the constant variety of animal sounds, the noise level was overtaking any thoughts in my mind. This dream became even more disturbing as the scary events from the past kept flashing in front of me getting in the way of my sight as I was trying to steer. This night was an image of me lying in bed over 25 years ago, waking up to what I thought was a stroke which ended up being Bell's palsy. A very scary time in my life, and I'll never forget it. My face was distorted and drooped on the left side; I couldn't see and could barely talk. Once arriving at the hospital, they said I was lucky to have gotten there as soon as I did. This was the time in my life when I had three miscarriages and made four moves out of state. Knowing that I was under a lot of stress at that time, it was no surprise how my body reacted, but to have it show up in my dreams puzzled me. The next image was when I had last been at the emergency room for anxiety. I saw myself lying on the hospital bed, talking with the nurse about changing my life choices. Then my dream shifted towards the animals; the owl sprung up from the back of the boat and flew onto my shoulder. He looked at me, then flew away, only to circle around me and come back to rest on the side of the ship, staring at me. Then the eagle flew out and circled around me and landed on the other side of the ship. Focusing on the sea in front of me, trying not to look at them, I could feel their eyes piercing me. As I kept steering ahead, I could hear the lion roar, and then a deep voice said," Look ahead; don't look back." Suddenly, a flash of lightning struck the front of the ship, and the owl and eagle were gone along with all of the other animals, and so was my sight. Blindness took the place of my sight, and as all of the noises had come to an end, fear and silence woke me up.

When I awoke the next morning, my eyes were sore but better, and I could open them. Being aware of how close I had come not just the day but many times before when I had damaged my eyes, my heart was filled with gratitude, and thankfulness consumed me. Waking up to powerful energy surging through me, I learned quickly to be grateful for everything because, truly, you are never promised tomorrow, nor do you know what it will bring. Immediately feeling blessed not losing my sight, I thanked God for allowing me to keep my sight; I then asked for guidance since I knew it was His voice in my dream that night. I picked up my Bible to look up anything I could find that might help with the animals that kept reoccurring in my dreams and in hopes He would guide my fingers to any other answers I was searching for. I was drawn to Psalms 102: 6-7, which says, "I am like a desert owl, like an owl among the ruins. I lie awake; I have become like a bird alone on a roof." Isaiah 40:31 says, "But those who hope in the Lord will renew their strength. They will soar on wings like eagles: they will run and not grow weary, they will walk and not be faint." Revelation 4:7 says, "The first living creature was like a lion, the second was like an ox, the third had a face like a man, and the fourth was like a flying eagle." then Daniel 7:4 says, "The first was like a lion, and it has the wings of an eagle. I watched until its wings were torn off, and it was lifted from the ground so that it stood on two feet like a human being, and the mind of a human was given to it."

<u>My Thoughts for Myself:</u>

Read 1 Thessalonians 5:16-18 daily - *"Rejoice always, pray continually, give thanks in all circumstances; for this is God's will for you in Christ Jesus."*

CHAPTER SEVENTEEN

My Proud And Not So Proud Moments

"Measure yourself by your best moments, not your worst. We are prone to judge ourselves by our moments of despondency and depression."

Robert A. Johnson

What if I try reframing my story like I had done with everyone else to find the good in myself, maybe I could switch my negative thoughts to good ones to better serve myself during this healing process. So, reflecting back to what positive moments I had in my life, the first thing that came to mind was being a good mother. As with anything, people seek guidance for step-by-step methods to help navigate any situation in life, and with our digital world, there are instant opinions, videos, and how-tos just waiting at our fingertips to know just how to do anything. As for me with my role as a mother, I stuck with my instinct (or gut feeling), heart full of love for them, and guidance only from God and the Bible. Even though I am not perfect and difficulties arose, I did the best I knew how to at the time with the best I was given and could give and provide. As with most children, they grow through the life of the adults they share it with, but ours got dragged through the good, bad, and ugly choices we made with no choice or voice. Knowing this early on, I did the best I could to help them understand everything we went through and why. Most parents avoid sharing anything bad with their children, only wanting them to experience rainbows and unicorns, but for me, it was important that my children knew the reality of good and bad situations in life to better prepare them for it all. I might not have had all the right answers, but I never strayed from making it my job to help them understand real-life situations to hopefully allow them to feel more comfortable as they grew up. Being a mother of three respectful well behaved boys is something any mother would be proud of. The only bad habit that they seem to have at this point in their lives is trying to break them from being so attached to their phones, some days more than others. We limit their time to help regulate that, but it's when they leave us to be with their other parents it becomes more of a free-for-all that we can't fight. I know if I had all that technology when I grew up, I might have had difficulties times controlling my usage as well. Since I'm a person who sits on the outside of the world, fighting the deep dark hole of a world driven by the need for high stimulation or distractions from life constantly, it was hard for me to relate until I understood better. Some days I would watch others tap in and out to run away from their reality just to seek enjoyment, which can be difficult to share a room with people who are so detached from each other. I'm not condemning or criticizing the people who do this; I just couldn't relate to their level sometimes, especially after my experience with yoga/meditation. Being aware or watching others too much caused me to be overly critical in situations that were unnecessary and none of my business. Now that my awareness and focus had changed on myself, not on others, I realized I had become one of them. My obsession with the digital world was learning how to heal and better myself, which seemed harmless since I was just listening to podcasts or books to learn more about my journey to help myself. Quickly did I see that the extreme amount of time I had given to my self-improvement project, I too, was detaching from everyone and the world around me. All these times, I had pointed out their extreme obsessions, and because I had never allowed myself to indulge in anything for any excessive amount of time, but here I was, falling into the same trap of distraction as everyone else. Even with it being good for me, there is still a need to have balance in your life with everything. We had put limits and boundaries on the boys, but I had not done that for myself. I might as well have said, "Do what I say, not what I do." what a poor example of self-control I had displayed. For the most part, I am pretty simple when it comes to needing any digital devices to make me happy or seek pleasure. When I needed a reset from life or an escape from reality, my preference was usually to participate in life, not run away from it. The time spent doing outside activities or with others was how I filled my need for pleasure and excitement. Considering everyone around me had changed their wants and needs from their lives, it affected my life since I had been accustomed to spending most of my free time with these other people. Now, I had to do most of this on my own, which at first was strange, but quickly, I learned I loved spending time with myself. This was much easier with the boys when they were younger, but as they grew up, it became harder to accept watching them turn into young men growing up and going their own way. With all my alone time, I could see the mirror of reflection displaying to me the digital junkie I had become as I spent hours after hours researching how to build my life back, an easy trap to fall into.

My oldest son is 18 and full of energy for life. Having a professional goal to achieve once he graduates, a daily routine that he keeps up with, and has figured out how to make time for the simple pleasures of life, which is amazing to understand at his age. Even though it's been a struggle for him to set boundaries with his time using digital devices, he has become much better at managing his time appropriately. He structures his life with all sorts of activities and other digital devices to bring enjoyment into his life. So he gets it and has figured out how to balance his own happiness along with sharing the happiness with others; his next step will be to incorporate life when he moves out into this balancing act. Where I'm starting back with myself and getting back my happiness to balance the scale I have tipped in the wrong direction. He didn't get there on his own, we have discussed life's turmoil through his eyes and mine. Together, we have encouraged each other and helped each other when no one else was there for us. I'm extremely proud of the young man he has turned out to be and even more proud of the mom I have become. He is an encouragement for anyone who meets him, with a great attitude that I admire. My other two sons are younger and if I continue on the path I have been as a mother so far, I'm hopeful that one day I'll have the same close relationship with each one of them as I have with my oldest. Here's the kicker as he moves on with his life I hope he retains what he has learned and keeps his healthy relationship with himself, but as for me being halfway through my life enough time has been wasted.

Through some of our decisions, we have discovered how our life is harder now because if you step back and really look at what there is to offer, you see it is so quick and fast that it is reasonable why people have become so easily bored and unsatisfied. All of our survival needs have been met, when we want to know something it's within seconds of our fingertips, no one has to leave their homes anymore to receive what they desire or want, so we are left with nothing to do so we search for something to do. Having so much additional time leads can lead to wasted time because the digital world is ready to fill those extra minutes with good and bad things if we are careful about what we choose. Just stopping to relax for some quiet time with yourself or spending time outside in nature to observe, would send most people into a state of guilt and anxiety for not staying busy or doing busy work. Here's where our "Monkey Mind" plays havoc, because we feel the need to feed the beast as I like to call it, if overload, it can ultimately create depression and sadness for some people if they overstimulate; we both had been there. While others might dabble in the experience because their brains don't require as much dopamine, they can become satisfied sooner before it gets out of hand. It takes a lot of self-control to balance your wants and needs without sacrificing some part of your life while making your "Monkey Mind" behave. Research has shown that the part of your brain that has pleasure is also connected to pain, and they are directly linked together. When the brain tips to pleasure, it must tip to pain to balance each other out; it's the law of physics. When we watch something pleasurable, the brain will shift to the other side of the pain, trying to balance the scale naturally, choosing to avoid the pain. We then move back over to the pleasure side and overindulge, craving more. Now, this causes a dopamine deficit state, which results in a lack of joy, irritability, anxiety, and insomnia because we have overindulged to receive such high rewards. In turn, we have now trained our brains to seek more and more only to avoid our pain and stay very distracted. Becoming aware can help balance the scale, get yourself back in control, and enjoy your life again without the need to fill it with short-term pleasures. After understanding why we have to balance our pain and pleasure sides to create a healthy mind, it was obvious I needed to get a handle on this before it consumed me and started to control me. Gaining control over what I could control was very important for not only my self-confidence but my self-control. Since there is so much in life we can't control, it seems foolish to not control what we can. This was among many things had I judged others before looking at myself first. Humbled by my awareness of falling into the same trap I judged others about; I was drawn to Matthew 7: 1-5. "Do not judge, or you too will be judged. For in the same way you judge others, you will be judged, with the measure you use, it will be measured to you. Why do you look at the speck of sawdust in your brother's eye and pay no attention to the plank in your own eye? How can you say to your brother, 'Let me take the speck out of your eye,' when all the time there is a plank in your own eye? You hypocrite, first take the plank out of your own eye, and then you will see clearly to remove the speck from your brother's eye." Returning to work after months of being off and the excitement of my new self-discovery, I was filled with happiness and beamed sunshine as I walked through the door. Everyone could see and feel my wonderful vibe; I was back to an old but better version of myself. People were drawn to my positive attitude, and I was overjoyed to share my experiences. Dancing and singing while I baked desserts and took care of customers during the day, I was a magnetic force no one could turn off. Life was great, and I felt amazing. All was good until one morning, all my love for life was met with a fierce desire to be angry, and everything I had enjoyed seemed to be taken away in a fleeting moment. Let me set the stage for what happened that morning. As with any normal Saturday morning at work, we were about to open up at 8:00 a.m. for breakfast. Among the many roles I play at our restaurant, I have been the breakfast cook for a few years. As usual, my routine was getting the kitchen set up and getting myself ready to start cooking; knowing that the next few hours I would be standing at the grill, I always made sure I went to the bathroom before we opened the doors for business. The bathrooms were outside of our restaurant in a lobby connecting us with some offices to the park we shared the building with. Most mornings before we opened, they would clean the bathrooms and mop the lobby way before we opened. By the time I went to the bathroom, they were usually done, but this morning, it was different. As I walked out into the lobby to make the turn towards the bathroom, I took one step and slid into the bench and into the janitor who was sitting on a bench right in front of the door. Landing right under his legs mangled, I had fallen flat down onto the hard floor, my right arm was extended above my head, I was drenched in a pool of water and my body was parallelized from the impact. My switch flipped instantly to anger, just a few days before I had been released from physical therapy getting a work-related injury on my left shoulder healed and working properly. Over time and the excessive amount of use my left shoulder had endured over the years, it became weaker and more difficult to use at times. After seeing the orthopedic doctor, his evaluation was to try physical therapy or change jobs to prevent further damage. While changing jobs was not an option; my only choice was to try physical therapy. Physical therapy worked and helped beautifully; until that morning. It was like taking your car to the shop to get a brand new paint job, every scratch and dent fixed and inside of it clean and shiny; only to pull away and get into an accident a few minutes later. All I could say at this moment was, "Damn it! It was my good side!" I was pissed off and mad as hell at him and the situation. The situation got more intense as his only words to me were, "Are you ok?" If I could have been able to move, I would have beat the sh** out of him for his lack of concern and lack of warning about the floors being wet. Thinking but never saying a word, "I thought, what do you think?" There was no sign where I walked out, and the only one out was on the other side of the lobby, where I couldn't see it. All it would have taken was for him to let me know the moment I opened the door that the floors were wet, but no, he just sat there watching me fall on my face. Lying there all twisted, rage was building inside me through the tremendous pain I was enduring; if we had locked eyes, he would have been mentally beaten to a pulp with the terrible thoughts that consumed my mind at that moment. Once getting to a point where I could get myself up with no help from him as he still just sat there clueless, I tried to make my way to the bathroom to dry off and evaluate the situation. By this point, everyone had been looking for me, and now I was the center of attention for help from everyone. Unfortunately, my disposition was nasty, which made me hard to deal with or communicate with, but once I completely stood up and allowed my body to try to move, my rage settled down a little as the pain was so overbearing all I could do was cry with every step I tried to take. This was worse than any car accident I had ever been through, and I have been through a lot of them. My right shoulder was stuck above my head and had come out of the socket, my head was locked and tilted to my left side, unable to budge, and I was unable to walk because my hips were twisted sideways; it was awful. I stood in front of the blow dryer in the bathroom, trying to dry my shirt, which was soaking wet from the floor; then the office ladies came in to help me. Having to discuss what happened immediately to them was their only interest because they were suddenly afraid of who was going to get blamed for this and have to pay for it.

Realizing their motives just made me madder by the minute, so I stopped talking and asked for my husband. After making my way back to the restaurant, I waited for the trip to the hospital to get checked out, and I asked my husband to handle it all. Fast forward a few months and many trips to a new physical therapist and orthopedic doctor, I was able to avoid surgery and was healing better than expected. It took over half of a year to recover both from my mental and physical state of mind, which completely shifted after this accident. I remembered reading a quote from J.M Barrie that says it all, "Life is a long lesson in humility."

<u>Quotes for Myself:</u>

"It's about humbling yourself enough to learn, even when you're at the top of your game. It's about knowing that the moment you get comfortable being an executive is the moment you begin to fail. It's about realizing that if you want to continue being Mufasa, at the same time, you have to keep being Simba."

Alex Banayan

"Being real is what keeps me humble. It doesn't matter how much money I make or how much I accomplish. What's critical is staying real to myself and keeping my feet on the ground. That's what helps keep me going."

Anuel A.A.

CHAPTER EIGHTEEN

Thank You For My Anger

"And once the storm is over, you won't remember how you made it through it, how you managed to survive, you won't even be sure the storm is really over. But one thing is certain, when you come out of the storm, you won't be the same person who walked in. That's what the storm is all about."

Haruki Murakam

When I visited my yoga teacher shortly after the accident; I explained what had happened and why I would not be able to participate in our sessions for a while. Since I thought my body was not 100% ready for a lot of the poses we had been doing, she explained turning our direction towards understanding where our body hurts and why would greatly benefit me especially after hearing the details of the accident. "Our bodies not only hurt from accidents that can occur but from our unhealed emotions that we carry", she declared. It was hard for me to have hope after this unexpected situation occurred, especially since I thought I had mastered accepting the things that were out of my control. She assured me I had much more to learn before assuming I was a master at anything, especially life. "Remember, you are always the student in life, and if you stop learning, you stop growing", she stated. I didn't want these unwanted emotional trespassers to continue making residence in my body, so I agreed to stay and go in this new direction for our sessions. She went on to say, "Once you fall into a depression realm, you lose creativity, happiness, and desire to enjoy anything in life; this is when your body needs to catch up to everything it had been introduced with and heal from it." Desperate to understand and to get relief, I listened carefully to what she was about to teach me. We went back to Louise Hay's book <u>You Can Heal Your Life;</u> she went through several of the areas I had pain with on our first visit. To my surprise, some of those pains were still present, and I had never truly addressed them like I thought. Fortunately for me, it was like learning how to ride a bike again. I just needed a refresher course, but this time, stay on the bike for the entire journey.

As we discussed my ailments, I began feeling like I was seeing a doctor, sharing my aches and pains, and waiting for the prescription to get rid of them. I rattled off every area of my body that was hurting, and she explained what emotion was behind each area of pain; it was like she could see right through me and inside my head with accuracy. Pain, in general, is from guilt, always seeking punishment; no wonder my body felt so much pain, considering the amount of guilt I had stored inside it. Curious, I shared some new present and past areas of pain, and she gave me her reasons why my body was suffering. My stiff neck represents rigid thinking, unbending flexibility, anger, and refusal to see other's side of the question; while the shoulders hold our burdens of life and lack of carrying out experiences in life joyously. My sore throat and laryngitis show that you're unable to express yourself and are too angry to speak. Having glaucoma, dry eyes, and almost losing my sight all clearly showed the inability to see the present, past, and future, along with reflecting pressures from long-standing hurts, stony forgiveness, and angry eyes from being overwhelmed by it all. The Bell's Palsy I went through was caused by an extreme amount of control over anger and an unwillingness to express feelings; that was exactly how I felt when that happened. Everything from my hip problems to my female issues was exactly how I was feeling; denial of self, lack of joy, fear of moving forward, anxiety, fear, and anger. Shortly after the accident, my bleeding came back, and a trip to the hospital followed next. Anger and stress seemed to be the common denominators here. I would single out an event or person to be angry at or blame them for what had taken place by them, which altered my mood and direction. I allowed them to have the steering wheel of my life and then proceeded to lose all of my self-control due to my built-up anger. The saddest part: no one ever knew, and when I changed my demeanor, I fell right into the pits with them, and it became my normal way to live. Even though I expressed my anger towards the janitor and anyone who would listen, it wasn't him I was angry at. It was the interruption in my life. Yes, he should have warned me about the floor, but placing blame for as long as I did over what happened affected me mentally and physically more in the long run.

Knowing that my body was finally in a pain-free place and my mind was at peace, being forced to start over again physically and mentally set off my anger to multiple levels that were unfamiliar to me. So I asked, "Why am I experiencing a different anger towards him?" After listening to me describing all of the feelings that I was going through involving the accident and my behavior towards everyone around, she concluded I had three types of anger rolling around inside me. My anger before was more of the silent type (keeping it all inside, never expressing it), so these expressive anger types were new. She explained each one, the cold rage which you have by expressing anger towards other's by turning them off or withdrawing from them physically and emotionally; hot anger, which displays facial and verbal gestures of anger outwards and is a behavior done in a hostile, aggressive way, and true rage is done with tunnel vision focusing on the source of the anger which increases your heart rate and puts you in a hyperventilated state of mind. No wonder everyone around me withdrew from me and was afraid to talk to me; my attitude and demeanor had changed drastically, and I would have been scared of me too. I had become the opposite of who I truly was: an unapproachable, miserable, and unhappy person out of control and mad at the world. After she described each one I had, she informed me that it takes less than 90 seconds to get angry and it takes around 23 minutes to react to an interruption that throws you off course, whether verbal interruption or life interruption. She followed up with, "As you were describing the accident to me right now and your feelings towards what happened, you took less than 10 seconds to become amped up with your anger and frustration. My anger before was just as scary because of my hidden, silent nature of holding anger in all of the time, but when I did let it out, I would get amped up, and no one saw it coming, and they could get annihilated very quickly. Holding all of this anger inside me was like holding the frog in the pot and slowly increasing the temperature as he continued to tolerate the heat, and when it quickly changed, he either was smart enough to jump out or he was faced with his own death. As for me, if I didn't (jump out) walk away to handle it within myself correctly, then everything around me usually died inside from my nasty outbursts.

As I am writing this book, a perfect example of both types of interruptions happened, but only one made me angry because I didn't set appropriate boundaries, which led to anger. Taking a break from writing, I decided to call my dear friend; I knew my window for conversation could be short or long, depending on what she had planned to do before work. As each day was different when she answered the phone, she would tell me my time frame to talk, and because I love to talk, I needed to be cut off sometimes. Knowing each other for so long, we have this understanding, and even though I got cut off on some days and not on others, it never made me angry. We respected each other's time and mental capacity to be in a place where we both could be heard, enjoy the conversation, and not feel obligated to appease each other. Don't get me wrong, we have venting calls and make time for those when needed, but we always respect each other's boundaries when doing so. Once I finished the call, I was exhausted from the information exchanged between us. So I decided to take a nap before returning to writing some more. As I lay there, my mind ran on what to write next, not uncommon these days since that has been what I have dedicated my time to. Conflicted on whether to get up and go write what I was thinking before I forgot it and being torn between allowing my brain to rest, I just sat in bed still thinking. Just about to get up and go write I had an interruption, someone needing an answer to a question right then. Even though they saw I was trying to sleep, they persisted to have a conversation with me. When they got the answer they needed they were done, and I was left forgetting all of the beautiful ideas I was anxious to go write about. Instantly anger flooded by body and mind from the interruption. Damn, I allowed myself to get anger over the exact thing I wrote about in the beginning of this chapter, then I became more anger now at myself. I got up paced back and forth desperately trying to remember my thoughts, only to come up blank. After 30 minutes of pacing a bright light over shadowed my dark thoughts.

Sorting it all in my mind this is what I came up with, maybe what I had been thinking wasn't meant to go in my book, but what just happened was. I've always said things happen for a reason here was my reason, to feel the anger and to figure out how to gain control before it got out of control. So I sat down in the middle of the floor, started deep breathing first inhaling then exhaling, and began meditating as I went through grounding poses to return to my center. Shortly after a few breaths, my control over the situation became easier to handle. Once I became centered in my body again, the message became clear. This honestly helped me realize how easily I can become angry over not setting appropriate boundaries, and how I could help myself regain my composure before it went too far. It wasn't about just getting interrupted it was about me losing my focus and becoming frustrated from it which led to my anger. What I should have done was stop the person before they spoke and said not right now and respected my head space, just like my friend and I do when we talk on the phone. It was my fault for getting so angry so fast, and not setting a boundary. After coming to this conclusion the ironic thing was even though I had gotten past being so angry so quickly, it left me with the adrenaline to get up, have the endurance to write this chapter, and the physical strength to do so despite my fatigue. Anger can provide fuel and power to accomplish a task when motivation can't, but it always takes a toll on our body and when it catches up to us if we don't take care of ourselves we can expect it to revolt. Doing the meditation helped me to release it from inside my body before the pain could settle in. Anger can sharpen your senses in the heat of the moment but it wrecks your brain, memory, and especially your body as you continue to hold it inside and never deal with it properly. G.K. Chesterton had a principle that says "change should not be made until reasoning behind the current state of affairs is understood. It says the rash move, upon coming across a fence, would be to tear it down without understanding why it was put up." As Mahatma Gandhi says, "Anger to people is like gas to the automobile – it fuels you to move forward and get to a better place. Without it, we would not be motivated to rise to a challenge."

Thinking back on how I dealt with my anger in the past by keeping it all inside I never embraced it or handled it; so this was a huge accomplishment for me to experience several emotions at once and have the skills to navigate through them in a healthy way. YEAH, ME! The old pattern of storing it and never addressing had been broken and obviously I had the right tools, now I needed the understanding behind so I redirected it when needed and made it my new pattern. So let's look at my anger and see how to see it through clear lenses. If I was threatened by anger, I would go into flight mode by shutting down and running away from the issue or fight mode which kicked in my survival mode which was where most of my anger stayed always fighting to stay in control and not appear helpless. For most people, this survival/fight mode turned their focus towards high energy and they needed to run away from the anger so they wouldn't have to deal with it in that present moment. They would withdraw from others, only look out for themselves, and drown themselves in anything and everything that has no connection to their current reality; meanwhile, all this was done with an incredible amount of adrenaline coming from their anger. When the outside world sees this, it can be terrifying to witness, and it instantly puts loved ones into flight or fight mode as well. This has happened to me before, and I reacted to how they acted in self-defense. Most of the time, my survival/fight mode did the opposite for me. I became anxious, losing my logic and creative senses, going numb to reality while my head would stay in a fog. I needed to react just like I did after my interruption early, acknowledge it, feel it, then embrace it and use it to fuel my drive towards a healthy energy to get rid of it; and to stop thinking or dwelling on it so I could allow it to turn into a challenge not a curse. Since the body increases respiratory functions and certain hormones kick in when anger strikes, it allows you to overcome what you're facing at a speed and strength you didn't realize you had. You get high energy and a self-confidence boost that increases your mental focus, which gives plenty of space for creativity and your pleasure senses, all of which are undeniably strong enough to prevent anger from settling in. So, in reality, I have experienced the shift from anger to a challenge, and I didn't even see it until now. Here is the best thing: after experiencing this shift from anger to calm, my bleeding stopped the very next day. Managing my anger and stress levels helped me control my bleeding; it was so crazy, but it worked. Learning how to move through an emotion by calming the brain through meditation taught me that I had more control than I imagined. When the incident happened with my husband's ex-wife due to her blind rage, it didn't scare the life out of me. It scared my life back into me, and without the life-threatening interruption, I would have never discovered my voice. Now, since the accident, I was introduced to how my anger can serve me, not hurt me. Oddly enough, these people deserve more than my forgiveness; they deserve my thanks and gratitude for opening my eyes to see the degree of my anger. Seeing my anger through my awareness, I was able to obtain my incredible power to know how to retrain and control my mind; nothing seems unattainable to me now. My power and strength have been inside me all this time; I'm so glad I finally found it. The key is to maintain it and never forget the lesson I learned from it.

<u>Quotes for Myself:</u>

"The more anger towards the past you carry in your heart, the less capable you are of loving in the present."

Barbara De Angelis

"Anger doesn't demand action. When you act in anger, you lose self-control."

Joe Hyams

CHAPTER NINETEEN

Finding Peace Within My Body

"Love yourself enough to walk into only the rooms and situations that show care and love for you. Love yourself enough to walk out of the rooms that harm you in any way. Love yourself enough to hold the people who harm you accountable for their words and actions. Love yourself enough to express your wants, your needs, and your desires. Love yourself enough to tell the truth. Love yourself enough to keep yourself safe. Love yourself enough to say enough is enough when enough has been enough."

Cleo Wade

Building my mobility and strength back into my body and retraining my mind was the focus. It was apparent that being grounded and centered, along with positive self-talk, was my next hurdle to overcome and that it also helped the healing of my body. Thinking back to our last yoga session, there was a part that piqued my curiosity: balancing your feminine and masculine energy. Knowing that we all have both feminine and masculine energy, your sex determines which one is predominant for us; it simply never occurred to me that they could get out of balance or have an impact on your body. She had said that the left side of the body represented our feminine energy, and the right side represented the masculine energy. It was my right side that stayed out of balance all the time ever since the accident. It was no coincidence that I had been showing some masculine traits through my anger. Doing the research excited me to understand exactly just how out of balance I was with either side; I was convinced it would help me become more centered and stay grounded. So here is what I found out about feminine energy. The feminine is all about receiving, taking in, and expressing anger and passion while being able to be supported, understanding, knowing her power, and being wise and compassionate. There was a whole lot more, but these were just a few that stuck out for me. For the feminine to become out of balance here is what shows up being depressed, needy, resentful, playing a victim role, being a people pleasure, the good girl, codependent, having low self-esteem, not wanting to be happy and putting everyone's needs before her own; some of these definitely hit home for me. Naming only a few, the balanced masculine energy shows up as strong, protective, confident, able to love unconditionally, powerful, passionate, empowered, and in touch with their feelings, but doesn't allow them to have control over themselves. The unbalanced masculine energy would have these characteristics: don't think of anyone else but themself, forceful, stubborn, endure and strive when it's time to rest, be headstrong, weak, cruel, disconnected with their emotions, ruthless, and disconnected with others and themself. It seemed obvious to me that my scales were in desperate need to be balanced before either side became more destructive. So, I made a list of what I had to work on to bring my feminine energy back up to where it belonged and a list of masculine traits that I needed to get rid of to help balance my scale. Making the list, I made sure I wrote beside each one a better way either how to incorporate it into my life or how to dispose of it from my life. Along with my list, I added some traits of my own to bring back into my life to rediscover my unique self; this would help me bring my sunshine and happiness back. This was not an easy task and one that would take a lot of work.

Keeping in mind to do the best I could and not to get discouraged if I failed, I made this a daily practice. I started reading them every morning and evening, and when I wrote in my journal, I made sure to keep myself in check. This was for me to have a healthy state of mind, returning back to my feminine side, which I had abandoned way too long, and also to help my body have the relief to heal better from the imbalance. Journaling had changed drastically for me over the years I wrote down my thoughts, thoughts for Ashley, my prayers, and any situation I couldn't get over. With all of the incredible knowledge I have received over the last few years, I adjusted my journaling to better suit my needs. Even though I still use it the same as before, it serves better purposes for me now. When I would get angry, depressed, anxious, or just needed to vent or work out a problem, I would run to my journal and write it all down; I still do that but with a follow-up on how to change or reframe the story or situation to better serve me and help me let go of it so I could move through it. So, writing down all of these new patterns that I have incorporated in life helps me stay on the right path, stay in my own lane, and is a reminder of just how important it is to do so. It also gives me peace inside to let it out in a non-threatening and more productive method, then I follow up with the necessary protocol and choose whether to move through in prayer, meditation, yoga, or an intense exercise to get the release that I need.

It's all about balance, balancing your life around what life throws at you. You can't just duck from it or run away from it because life is like a boomerang. It will keep coming back until you are forced to pick it up or catch it; either way, you will see it again. I decided to put everything on a scale of wants and needs and look at it from two perspectives: what I personally wanted and needed in my life and what I didn't want and need in my life from others, situations I was in that needed attention for myself, then visualize it. This would create a healthy balance for my future and allow my mind to shift towards a goal to achieve a more positive outcome. Considering no one can predict the future, and as we all know, everything and everyone changes constantly, this would be my challenge to maintain a life of balance, weathering all of the stormy days that will arise from day to day. Next, I needed to acknowledge all of the bad habits and negativity I had picked up along the way in my life that I had consumed from my past and discard them like trash. This brings me to a story that my dear friend shared with me about the example she had recently used on how to get rid of all the bad energy from situations that happened in the past and the bad patterns. She was explaining to me about a family member of hers who was having trouble letting go of their terrible past and moving away from it so it would stop interrupting their present day. After much discussion and forth between them, she couldn't get the message across on how necessary it is to eliminate the past from our minds so we can move forward in life and let go to enjoy our present. So, in order to get her point across, she used this illustration to better explain. I warn you, this example she used is kinda gross, graphic, and disgusting, especially for me to write it in my book, but I promise once you hear it, you'll understand its relevance. Imagine you have the worst case of constipation that has lasted for several days, and when your body is finally ready to release it, you run to the bathroom to get relief. The release is so freeing, and you begin to feel normal again. After you're done and have handled your business, you're ready to get up, clean up, and move on. Your first instinct is to flush it away; you don't look at it, you don't smell it, and you don't leave it. You might thank it for the relief, but you certainly don't want it hanging around. That is how our past is, you might thank it for finally showing you to receive a lesson from it, but you don't need to keep looking at it or feel the need to have it hang around like a nasty reminder.

Your body is always internalizing everything good and bad; we give it and store it inside. In the example, our body needs relief and release from holding in our past and demands a clean vessel just like the toilet did. Since we mirror everything our body holds from the inside to our outward appearance, would you want to look like the nasty stuff you're holding inside? I don't! So I took her example and used it to dispose of every nasty thought, situation, and memory that I had been carrying, but I didn't flush them; I burned them away. I wrote them all down on index cards, sat on the floor, and placed them all around me. Similar to what I had done in my dream about the bottles that had messages inside them, I revisited each one, acknowledged their significance, went through every emotion and feeling that they had given me, and then burned each card. By burning them, I was choosing to free my mind from them; this was empowering for me and the best way I could finally let them go. It was just like her bathroom story; I walked in, sat down, and got relief from the nastiness inside, and then discarded them.

The next turning point was accepting that I had spoken enough truth to have become aware that it was time to start working on myself away from my mind and into my body to completely be healed from my past. Stealing moments here and there helped me grow even more. Being able to take 10 to 20 minutes in meditation when needed to escape life's difficulties was priceless. This allowed me to rest at any time of the day and return with a better mindset. Mindset and yoga go hand and hand because if you can regulate your body first, then you can regulate your mind. You can't regulate your mind first because it lies to you all of the time, but your body can't lie to you. When your body is hurting, you feel it, and you know it. Breathing is a key component in that process; when you breathe slowly, you can calm down and get relaxed. Did you know that nasal breathing has a positive effect on your cognitive functioning? Part of your cognitive functioning is linked to your brain, which, if properly working, gives clarity, and in return, you have positive thinking. Positive thinking helps us have a better mindset, which doesn't allow room for negativity. Positive thinking came easy to me most of the time, it was having a positive attitude when in the company of negative energy that would zap my mood and change my direction. As I developed better self-talk by changing the bad thoughts to good thoughts as they ran through my mind, positive thinking started taking over anything negative that tried to get in. I was able to turn away any unapproachable or unpleasant situations that surrounded me into a more positive and productive way to handle them. Learning how to be grounded and centered helped me have balance to have a more positive outlook on my life, which helped me control my emotions better, which in turn gave me self-confidence and less anxiety.

<u>Quotes for Myself:</u>

My destination is no longer a place, but rather a new way of seeing.

Marcel Proust

Letting go – at some point, you have to let go and move on. It might be the hardest thing in the world you do, but you have to summon all of the strength you possibly can to finally let go. Some people and things just aren't going to be meant for you, no matter how much you wish they were. Some jobs and situations just won't work out, no matter how much you hoped they would. But know that it's okay for things to not work out. Nobody's life is a straight line that makes perfect sense. Everybody has twists and turns, and everyone has to turn around every now and then. So when you find yourself wishing and hoping things out of your control will change, summon all of your strength to let go and start heading in a new direction because it will lead you closer to your new path.

Nikki Banas

CHAPTER TWENTY

Connecting With My Chakras

"Opening your chakras and allowing cosmic energies to flow through your body will ultimately refresh your spirit and empower your life."

Barbara Marciniak

Sharing my dream about Ashley with my yoga teacher gave her a new direction for our future sessions. Learning about chakras was our upcoming discussions, along with foundational poses for developing balance and strength. According to Wedmd.com, the definition "Chakra is a Sanskrit word that means wheel or cycle. There are seven main chakras situated along the spine, from the base of your spine to the crown of your head." According to a website named Higherselfing.com, the definition "Chakras, by definition, are wheels; they are energy vortexes within the human body that help regulate all its processes, from organ function to the immune system and the balancing of energy." Chakras intrigued and fascinated me; they were an additional way to control both your body and mind.

Exploring deeper into them, I discovered that there are animals that are associated with each one. Finding out as much information as possible, my research helped me identify my dreams and their meanings. We took each chakra one by one; she explained what they represented and which poses were used to help unblock them. I have listed each one, what blocks them, and how to unblock them. The seven chakras are root, sacral plexus, solar plexus, heart, throat, third eye, and crown.

Root Chakra – The root chakra is located at the base of your spine at your tailbone and governs your legs and feet; this is your grounding foundation. This should be your starting point when unblocking chakras because it maintains your entire energy system, and if the root chakra is blocked, you can guarantee all of the other chakras will be as well. Having an overactive chakra will produce anxiety and fear, and one that is underactive will disconnect you from the outside world. This energy, when balanced, will provide stability, security, growth, courage, good health, and the ability to stay in the present moment. When the root chakra is unbalanced, you can become depressed, have an inability to focus or learn, and will be highly sensitive to light, sound, or your environment, and your fight or flight mode is more likely to kick in. The poses related to unblocking the root chakra are garland pose, chair pose, and warrior pose. In our sessions, we always began with the lotus pose and worked our way into the other poses after stretching every part of our body, which allowed us to become grounded. When we did slow meditative poses, we would chant for the chakra we were focusing on in that pose. The chant for the root chakra is "LAM" or saying "I Am." At first, chanting felt silly, but once I went into a meditative state, I became very comfortable and noticed how well it helped me to fall into a relaxing and spiritual peace of mind. Some questions to ask yourself to help balance in this chakra would be: Where do you get your courage and stamina from? Can you recall feeling stable in the past? Do you have the basics covered, such as shelter, food, water, and the ability to obtain what you need in time of crisis? When the Root Chakra is balanced our life lesson should be to feel safe and secure in our physical life, maintain good health and sexuality, and manifest our basic needs.

Sacral Plexus Chakra – The sacral plexus is located two inches below your navel and is connected to your digestive system and the adrenal glands. The physical issues when the sacral plexus is out of balance are sexual and reproductive issues, urinary problems, and kidney issues. Since this chakra is located in the stomach region, it regulates your sense of power and pleasure, gut feelings, well-being, and creativity; if out of balance, you will experience fears, anxiety, loss of control, and have eating disorders. When balanced, the sacral plexus has the ability to enjoy senses of pleasure, creativity, and having healthy relationships; but when it's unbalanced, all of those go into lockdown mode along with being unable to express emotions and having insecurities. Doing hip-opening poses helps restore and unblock this chakra, poses like spinal twists, warrior pose, crescent pose, and cat-cow pose. The chant for the sacral plexus to release and heal is "VAM" or "I Feel." Some questions to ask yourself to help balance in this chakra would be; can you relax enough to participate in a celebration of life to give thanks for all you see and enjoy? Do you honor your body's need for rest when you're tired? Do you complicate your life with too much mental activity? When our Sacral Plexus Chakra is balanced, our life lesson should be to feel free to create healthy boundaries, express creativity, and connect with others through our emotions without losing our identity.

Solar Plexus Chakra – The solar plexus is all about feeling in control of your life and being confident; in essence, it is your power. Its fiery center fuels courage, energy, motivation, and decision-making and is goal-oriented. Too much fire energy can create the impulse to react in anger or aggression. Since this chakra is at our center, it manages our life energy to maintain balance in our mind and body. An overactive solar plexus chakra will experience a desire to control everything and judge too harshly, which can overstimulate your system to an overwhelming amount of negative energy. Anxiousness, guilt, and shame show up here and are the main sources of your pain; these types of pain are in the gastric system, which causes nausea or vomiting during an episode of anxiety. Trauma, abuse, or any emotional abuse will damage the solar plexus, which can cause some areas to shut down internally. The poses to unblock this chakra are a downward dog, camel pose, plank pose, bow pose, and boat pose, and more beneficial while chanting "RAM" or "I Can" either silently or out loud. Some questions to help balance this chakra would be; do you know that you are always free to choose in every situation? Are you willing to express yourself in a powerful way that lets others know not to mess with you? Do you hide your innate sense of worth from others because you think you will be different? When Solar Plexus Chakra is balanced, our lesson should be experiencing the depth of who we are through self-empowerment and self-esteem so we can live out our life's tasks and soul purpose.

Heart Chakra – In the center of your chest at heart level is the heart chakra; it's all about connecting and relating to your energetic center through receiving and giving love to yourself and others, which in turn opens us up to having better relationships. The heart chakra grants unconditional love, gratitude, compassion, kindness, and forgiveness when in balance and can enhance empathy, which will give a deeper understanding of others and their experiences. When this chakra is out of balance, the emotional issues that show up are feeling disconnected, jealousy, being guarded, depression, hopelessness, and you feel heaviness and become stuck, loss of self or a loved one, grief, and hurt will develop as well. The physical symptoms are immunity issues, heart and lung issues, poor circulation, the tension in shoulders and neck, heart palpitations, and chest pain; as with most of the other chakras, anxiety or PTSD can show up here as well. The poses to unlock the chest and activate the heart chakra are wheel pose, cobra pose, bridge pose, and fish pose. For the chant that helps with this chakra, you would say "YAM" and "I Love You." Some questions to help balance the heart chakra would be; can you forgive those who hurt you in the past? What makes your heart sing and gives you joy? How do you define joy, and what does it feel like? Where do you find joy in your life? When your heart chakra is balanced, our lesson is to have a peaceful equilibrium through practicing gratitude, love, compassion, appreciation, and forgiveness, along with experiencing connection with self and others.

Throat Chakra – Traveling up from your chest to the center of the neck is the throat chakra, the central communication hub of the body. The throat chakra is all about sound and speaking truth for both internal and external expression of self. Fear of expressing feelings for any reason and experiencing challenges around communication, along with silencing your voice or rearranging words to suit other people's reactions, will not only shut you down but are the main reasons this chakra gets blocked. An unbalanced throat chakra will cause depression, anxiety, and low self-esteem; the physical effects are stiffness and pain in the neck, thyroid problems, dental issues, sore or hoarse throat, mouth ulcers, and jaw problems. When this chakra is balanced, you find your voice, speak your truth, sing praises, be expressive, have faith and hope, and have good, clear communication. The poses associated with this chakra are plow pose, cat pose, lion pose, and shoulder stand pose. This chakra's chant is "HAM" and "I Speak." Some questions to help balance the throat chakra would be; where do you channel your creative energy? Do you know when it is appropriate to be silent? Do you always need external noise to keep you from your thoughts? Do you feel that telling the truth may be offensive to others? When your throat chakra is balanced, our lesson is to give yourself room to grow and expand and use your beauty and authentic self to express and speak your truth through your purpose, which will unfold out of you the moment you free it.

Third Eye Chakra – The third eye is located between your eye and the energy vortex in the center of your forehead. It is considered your sixth sense – your wisdom, your imagination and intuition, your higher consciousness and emotional healing. The third eye plays as an internal screen where memory, images, dreams, and fantasy are displayed with complete focus and clarity. If unbalanced, you feel lost, adrift, confused, have a busy mind, stressed, anxious, have intrusive thoughts or memories and nightmares, and are prone to negative thinking and limiting beliefs. Once your third eye loses its inner wisdom, you feel stuck day to day, your brain and eyes will develop health problems, and you can't trust your own opinions to make decisions. The poses for this chakra are child pose, lotus pose, thunderbolt pose, and downward facing dog pose; for this chakra, the chants are "OM" and "I See." Some questions to help balance the third eye chakra would be; in your wisdom, can you forgive the past and extract the learning that was there for you? Do you let others drain you because you cannot discern a healthy boundary or want to please others? Can you trust your intuition when it tells you about someone or something? Can you imagine being loved and cherished in a way that respects who you are? When your third eye chakra is balanced, our lesson is to become wise in a productive way, enjoy the balance of our beautiful reality and dream world, use our imagination to better serve us, and maintain healthy physical abilities.

Crown Chakra – The crown chakra is located at the top of your head, representing your connection to spirit, the Divine, and God, and rules the external forces of your individual reality. It is known to be the gateway to your higher power and enlightenment, where you can fully trust your inner wisdom. This chakra deals with our inner and external beauty, our bliss, happiness, and intelligence. When balanced, we can be open-minded and have the ability to ask the necessary questions freely, and the ability to assimilate and analyze information properly. When the crown chakra is blocked, we lose the ability to connect with spirit, ourselves, and others; we feel isolated and out of touch with anything outside of ourselves. We will live in our heads, have excessive attachments or addictions, feel confused or depressed, and have a rigid belief system that allows for a closed mind and an unsatisfied life. The tension from this blockage will produce intense pain around the forehead and temples, pressure behind the eyes, and even pain through the entire body. Some physical symptoms from this chakra being blocked are brain fog, lack of either not enough sleep or poor sleep patterns, fatigue and physical exhaustion, poor coordination, and sensitivity to light or sound. The poses for this chakra are corpse pose, headstand pose, forearm stand pose, and rabbit pose; combine these with meditation and the chants "OM" and "I See," and this chakra will open up with a sense of empowerment and awareness to your soul and body to make a spiritual connection. Some questions for the crown chakra would be: Do you allow your own beauty and light to shine? Do you need to receive anything in order to feel your bliss? Do you need others to change in order for you to feel your bliss? Can you open yourself to the love, guidance, and protection of a greater force rather than limiting yourself? When your crown chakra is balanced, our life lesson is to experience peace of mind and to experience the meaning of life through the Divine.

Through one of our many meditations, there was one that revealed the flower that had shown itself many times in my dreams. It was the lotus flower, which represents the crown chakra because both are associated with enlightenment, spiritual rebirth, and growth; it was ironic to learn both had aligned with my healing. The lotus flower is an aquatic plant that grows in slow-moving water, hence the slow process too healing. They are found in ponds and river deltas in Asia, India, China, and Vietnam. They are symbolic of purity, strength, and resilience because they rise with their bloom from the mud without stain every day and return when the day is back to the murky water, and no matter the environment, they remain perfectly clean. This is the best example of awakening and letting go of our darkness to embrace the radiance of our light, no matter what the external world issues you might be faced with.

<u>Quotes for Myself:</u>

"Like the lotus flower that is born out of mud, we must honor the darkest parts of ourselves and the most painful of our life's experiences because they are what allow us to birth our most beautiful self."

Debbie Ford

"I have had dreams, and I've had nightmares. I overcame the nightmares because of my dreams."

Jonas Salk

CHAPTER TWENTY ONE

From Dreams To Reality

"There is a mystical, wondrous world inside you awaiting your invitation to awaken and express itself. Cosmic dances, celestial songs, and dreams with colors and storylines of the grandest glory. So go ahead – drop the chains of limitations, strip down to the raw beauty of your truth and essence, release your magical self, and experience a life so splendidly exciting you will wonder why you choose to allow your mystic heart to remain in slumber for so long"

Zahrah Sita

Since Ashley had been speaking to me every night for years, captivating my thoughts and trying to bring clarity to my mind, her guidance had allowed me to have a whole new perspective in a way to reframe my stories to heal instead of hurt and let go instead of the holding the past to allow my emotional wounds to heal. I began looking forward to bedtime now that my dreams were becoming a vital role in my healing. It didn't matter if they were bad or good; each one led to a new discovery in my life. Our roles changed from time to time; she was me, and I was her until finally, I revealed myself to her. Along with learning about chakras and their connection to healing my body, it was interesting when I discovered that certain animals were represented with each chakra that had been in my dreams and played a significant role in my understanding of how to deal with my past. Almost all my dreams during this time frame were on a beach surrounded by water or had taken place in the ocean; considering my thoughts and emotions, I knew my conscious and subconscious were sorting through a hodgepodge of my memories. In dreams, the beach represents our personal growth and a need for relaxation to create an emotional balance, and because of its ever-changing nature, the ocean reflects our emotional state of mind through the details of each movement. When I was swimming against the current, it meant big challenges were ahead, and when I washed up onto the shore, it was about unfamiliar situations that were about to take place. The confusion behind questions like "Where am I?" and "Why am I here?" would show up countless times while I was going into the water or coming out. The waves crashing were showing how to navigate through the challenges of life, and to learn how to use ebb and flow to ride the waves instead of fighting them. Rough waves showed up as lessons needed to be processed. Traveling back to my oldest and longest reoccurring dream about the little girl on the beach, by interpreting the details, animals, and scenery, plus my new knowledge of chakras, I began seeing the full context of my dream.

The Dream - Smell the salty air as it blows through the coastal sand dunes. The heat of the bright sun radiating down you feel the heat of the sparkling white sand between your toes. Looking above the crystal blue sky you see it filled with a variety of gorgeous birds gliding around. In the distance is an elephant stumbling as he tries to walk down the beach. Look closer you see a swarm of bees surrounding him. He begins to swat fiercely with his trunk back and forth, trying to keep them off him. As you look to the side of him, you notice beautiful butterflies fluttering around boxes, some half opened and some half closed, scattered around surrounded by lotus flowers. Shifting your attention to the other side of the beach, you see a little girl playfully bouncing up and down the shoreline. She was watching dolphins play in the water. As they jumped in and out of the water, you could hear her musical laugh echo across the waves. Suddenly she took off toward an old abandoned fun park. As she began running down the beach, she looked back and said, "Come find me!" As she enters the park, she heads into the house of mirrors. Following her inside, you become aware that every mirror is broken, with many different sad images of the girl displayed on each one. You begin to glance from mirror to mirror, confused. Suddenly she vanishes. Your heart begins to race, searching for her. As you touch each mirror, realize the faces switched to your reflections. You begin to panic. Abruptly, a scared and trembling voice cries out and says to you, "Help find me!" You feel a sharp pain in your chest, which is familiar as it rushes through, realizing it is a panic attack from anxiety. This had become a common part of your daily life but never in your dreams. You close your eyes tightly and take a deep breath. Opening your eyes all you see is darkness. As you begin to feel your way around the slick surfaces, a door opens. Walking through it, you notice the sand between your toes is cold, not warm. The sun was no longer shining. The sky was gloomy, with eagles and hawks flying over the still waters. There is the elephant trying to walk down the beach, but instead of fighting off bees, it is wasps swarming him.

There were no beautiful butterflies for him to walk by, only dead flowers along with the scattered half-opened and half-closed boxes with blood oozing from them. Horrified, you look away to the opposite side of the beach. Catching a glimpse of thrashing in the water, you move toward it to get a better look. There was the little girl crying and staring at crocodiles fighting with each other in the rough waters.

As you draw near, she turns towards you and says, "Please find me before it's too late! Alarmed, you freeze, and black dust begins to swirl around you and carries it all away. Remember the elephant first walking on the beach with a swarm of bees around him, then the bees switched to wasps? Since the root chakra is connected to our memory, it only makes sense that one of the animals representing it would be an elephant since they're known to never forget. While elephants are known to be big, strong, and stable, they also have the largest brains in the animal kingdom. They are born with a large cerebral cortex which stores an incredible amount of memory. Elephants have thick, tough skin to protect them from predators. Of course, they are not bulletproof, but they are afraid of bees mostly due to the consistent buzzing noise they make. Think about that for a minute: one of the largest creatures on the planet is afraid of a tiny insect. After coming across some interesting facts about elephants and how they represent strength and happiness and are promoted by nature to be protective of their families, it only seemed fitting that an elephant showed up in my dreams. Speaking for the root chakra, the elephant displays great stability with a firm foundation. The need for grounding and balance was represented by the sandy beach he traveled on; even though he stumbled, he never fell or moved off course. We must learn to stand strong as we move through life, not allowing the annoyances around us to disturb our presence, which allows us to be fully grounded and be present in the moment. The bees seemed to be the interruptions in life, trying to take the attention off the task at hand. When they are in our dreams, bees are said to be symbols for change, and their buzzing sound is said to remind us to trust miracles because the celestial humming is what leads us in the direction of moving forward in life. The Toltecs believe when dreaming about bees, it is the need to see all living things co-exist in peace, community, love, and harmony, which is why they are connected to the heart chakra as well. Once the wasps showed up, they were annoying insects that gave insight into the trouble ahead, and when they showed up in our dreams, they represented anger, negativity, and confrontation. They were examples of the harmful things that show up in our lives to hurt or distract us from following our desired path, and if we are not careful they could detour us and cause just enough chaos to change our direction. I had been guarded my entire life, not having a direct path of my own, only following the path of others and stumbling the entire way. The elephant continued his path, confident in his own leadership, handling it with grace despite the annoying interruptions he had to face; he never missed a step and just kept walking. Much like the elephant, I wasn't bulletproof either, even though I had built a strong wall around myself for protection. No matter how big and strong the elephant was, he could not control what was happening around him, but he did have control over his reactions. This was no different than us trying to control life when it happens outside of us; it is our reaction to it that will determine how we handle it. You can't control others or what happens around you. Everyone is in their own head space for which no one knows of another thoughts or intentions, and change occurs every second of every day. Being taught to be seen, not heard, it was difficult to separate myself from anything that tried to penetrate my protective shield. Drawn like the bees and wasps to the elephant, the outside world had slowly been annoying my every step, but where he had control over his reactions, I had to learn how to control mine.

Before taking our attention to the little girl enjoying watching the dolphins in the water, let us acknowledge the eagles flying in the sky. In our dreams, eagles and hawks are sent to let us know we need to look at things with a discerning eye. The Eagles are said to be connected to God; this was my friendly reminder to reconnect with God. When they bring their energy into a dream, it is to help with focus leadership and protection from threatening situations. Eagles also send messages of major steps in our life that are about to take place; and the insight to prepare for them. Back to the little girl and the dolphins, they represent the fun and enjoyment that needed to find its way back into my life. With their kid-like play, it's a reminder that we should be living a life full of joy and creativity to ensure harmony and balance. Unlike the crocodile that later took the dolphins' place in the water, the fun stopped immediately and quickly shifted to chaos and fear of the unknown when that exchange happened. When this animal appeared in my dream, it disturbed boundaries, caused anxiety, and threatened life, just like the people and events from my past had done. When life is happy and going well, it's the negative outside world that can flush all your fun away if we allow it. My fun-filled, positive life and free-loving spirit had turned dark and gloomy, full of displeasure when attacked by threatening sources of negative energy, but now with my understanding of mindfulness and a new mindset, I know that they were doing the best with what they knew how to do at that the time and holding any anger was pointless. Blaming or judging others was never the right answer; forgiveness and love were the solutions that came easy when I learned how to have gratitude for everything. Spending time in gratitude helped me realize there was never a need to understand why things happened, what I needed to understand was how to handle them with grace and use my femininity to encompass a passionate and nurturing behavior towards people and the situation.

Let's shift our attention towards the butterflies fluttering around the empty boxes. Butterflies are known for transformation, rebirth, and growth, and one of the animals represents the throat chakra. As I was evolving into the person I was meant to be, new beliefs and thoughts were developing along with my new attitude and my voice. By following her cries, "Come find me!" "Help find me!" and "Please find me before it's too late!" my direction shifted to myself instead of her, and I realized the importance of finding and helping myself before it was too late. Peeling layer by layer off, realizing this would be a lifetime journey, I was ready for the challenge and excited for the change. Each layer allowed me to feel closer to my true authentic self. Just like the caterpillar needs time to metaphor into the beautiful butterfly that it will become, so did I need time to feel and heal. As time passed, I couldn't understand why people couldn't see things the way I saw things in life or the many changes that distracted us from following our desired path, and if we were not careful they could detour us and cause just enough chaos to change our direction through. When I asked my yoga teacher, her answer was, "You are becoming the butterfly and they are still in the cocoon waiting to evolve. No one can see your stage until they have been in your stage and come through it." When the boxes changed from being empty to oozing blood and the butterflies were gone then replaced with dead flowers, it was time to face that part of my past. My dreams had revisited with each and every pregnancy that had entered my body. When I took them one by one and re-lived their arrival and departure, I could feel their love and finally be at peace with my closure for that part of my life. This was an emotional time for my mind and body, and I thank God for my yoga teacher who guided me through this painful process. She taught me how to feel every emotion sit with it through meditation, and finally release and let it go. Letting go was difficult with many parts of my past, but I knew the only way to be present and move toward my future was to finally let things go. The way I finally knew I had completely let go was when I would look at the person or situation that had triggered me and it didn't have an effect on me anymore; then and only then could peace come into my heart and not pain or anger. She gave me a statement I will never forget, "Think of a piece of Swiss cheese, let go of what needs to go through the holes, and what you're meant to keep will stick and stay." What a great and simple example, from then on I consciously thought of what needed to stay and what needed to go. Even though some situations haven't been that easy to simply let go, what I have learned is that it is necessary to follow through with however short or longer the process might take, but you can't keep what doesn't serve you. For me meditation has been my best source of releasing any negative emotions that try to take residence in my mind, some days are easier than others but I persist and remember the torture from all of the years I suffered unnecessarily, and tell myself "I won't repeat that nasty cycle." My only regret is that I didn't heal sooner in my life, but we all know God has a plan and things happen for a reason and at His pace, not ours. So with that being said I am grateful for all I have experienced good and bad in my life. Who knew that a book intended for the daughter I never had would be exactly what I needed to become the woman God wanted me to be? Taking this leap into my new adventure has been an eye-opening process, life-changing, and a complete game-changer for me; for which I am eternally grateful for my yoga teacher/mentor/friend. She is a truly inspiring woman and a gift from God. My life will forever be uplifted by the knowledge and time she shared with me. By this point in my life, forgiveness has taken place, gratefulness has shown up, and anger has been burned away. In the days to come, you will find me resting in the metamorphism stage, learning more until time to share my next journey. As I continue to transform into a beautiful butterfly ready to explore my newfound world and into the amazing woman God made me.

<u>Quotes for Myself:</u>

"Healing is a different type of pain. It's the pain of becoming aware of the power of one's strength and weakness, of one's capacity to love or do damage to oneself and to others, and how the most challenging person to control in life is ultimately yourself."

Caroline Myss

"Let today be what today needs to be. Whether you travel through quickly or slowly, breathe deep, no matter your pace. Take action where you need to take action, and if a moment calls for stillness, then embrace stillness. You are allowed to welcome the ebb and flow. You are allowed to pace yourself through every unknown one day at a time. One hour at a time. Perhaps you will find there is grace to make it through this, just fine."

Morgan Harper Nichols

95